TEACHING YOUR CHILD TO LOVE LEARNING

A GUIDE TO DOING PROJECTS AT HOME

TEACHING YOUR CHILD TO LOVE LEARNING

A GUIDE TO DOING PROJECTS AT HOME

Judy Harris Helm

Stacy Berg

Pam Scranton

TEACHERS COLLEGE, COLUMBIA UNIVERSITY
NEW YORK AND LONDON

Published by Teachers College Press, 1234 Amsterdam Avenue, New York, N.Y. 10027

Library of Congress Cataloging-in-Publication Data

Helm, Judy Harris.
   Teaching your child to love learning : a guide to doing projects at home /
Judy Harris Helm, Stacy Berg, Pamela Scranton
      p. cm.
   Includes bibliographical references and index.
   ISBN 0-8077-4471-9 (pbk. : alk. paper)
    1. Education-Parent participation. 2. Activity programs in education.
   3. Motivation in education. 4. Home and school. I. Berg, Stacy M.
   II. Scranton, Pamela. III. Title.
LB1048.5.H45   2004
306.874-dc22   2003068744

ISBN 0-8077-4471-9 (paper)

Printed on acid-free paper
Manufactured in the United States of America
07 06 05 04 03 02 01 00 8 7 6 5 4 3 2 1

Dedication

We dedicate this book to our own children—Lauren, Joey, Alex, Drew, Seth, Jena, Amanda, and Rebecca—for being all they are and allowing their stories to be shared, and to our husbands—Sean, Andy, and Rich—for supporting us in our work. Without the joy of learning and loving in our own families, we would have nothing to share.

Acknowledgments

We always count as a source of our knowledge and strength Lilian Katz, who has taught the world about what is worthwhile and beneficial for children and how to make it happen through project work. She is a personal mentor and supporter, and we feel enormously blessed by her appearance in our lives. Likewise Mary Ann Gottlieb, who inspires us as she continues to grow and search for what is best for children even in retirement. The staff and congregation of Northminster Presbyterian Church have supported our work in so many ways. We are thankful for the work of Rebecca Wilson for both translating materials into Spanish and providing so many excellent ideas and for her colleague Laura Bradfield for her input. We are also extremely appreciative of the extra time and effort Susan Liddicoat at Teachers College Press put in to teach us how to make our writing meaningful for parents.

We are grateful to those who provided input in parenting classes, those who read the book and gave feedback, and those who participated in the field testing of the project journal. These include teachers, children, and families from Discovery Preschool, West Liberty Dual Language Prekindergarten Program, Rockford Early Childhood Program, and Rock Island Head Start. Their suggestions and refinements kept us focused on what would be useful for parents and families. We are especially grateful to those families who participated in parenting classes and were generous in sharing their children's work in this book. These include, Luz and Martin Niño and their children Concepción and Ervin; Rod and Lisa Perdue and daughter Audrey; Christina Walshire and son Joshua; Linda McClain and daughter Elizabeth; Cherie Hoefft and children Ashley and Ryan; Julie Rivera and daughter Aimee; Andy and Jennifer Haines and daughter Kathryn; Amy Sanders and son Reed; Jenny Schellenberg and sons Caleb, Josh, and Matthew; Mimi Fox and Joel Swenor and their son Gordon; Terra Shelton and daughter Caroline; Mary Ann Gottlieb and grandson Atticus; Jesus and Nanette Chapa and daughter Nanette; and Jennifer Loer and daughter Kaylin.

Contents

Preface

So you want to raise children who love to learn! If you do, we think you are probably interested in using the project approach! Maybe as a parent you are concerned that your child isn't interested in school or doesn't seem to care about learning how to read and write or other academic subjects. Maybe you are looking for something to get your child unplugged from the TV or video games. Maybe you have read some articles on brain research and want to know if you can help your child be smarter. Or perhaps your child's teacher uses the project approach in her classroom and you have seen the benefits. Maybe you are a parent of a home-schooler and are looking for a way to use meaningful learning experiences to integrate your curriculum. Whatever your interest, we are excited that you want to learn more about how to use project work with your child. Whether you are a parent, grandparent, caregiver, or another important person in the life of a young child, we feel the project approach can provide meaningful opportunities for you to spend quality time with your child while helping him learn and develop a variety of skills.

Who We Are

We, the authors of this book, are both educators and parents. Judy Harris Helm owns her own educational consulting company and is a former teacher, director, and college professor. Her two girls are now grown: one is a bilingual teacher, and the other is working toward a doctorate degree.

Stacy Berg is the director of Northminster Learning Center, a faith-based, child-focused center providing toddler and preschool educational programs and after-school care. Stacy is the mother of an infant daughter and two sons, ages 3 and 5.

Pam Scranton is a preschool teacher at the Northminster Learning Center and mother of a daughter, age 16, and two sons, ages 6 and 12.

Projects and Families

As professionals, we use the project approach in our classrooms and train other teachers in how to use it. As parents, we have also become wrapped up in projects as we encouraged our own children's interests. We cherish memories of favorite family projects. Often when parents have shared with us their concerns about raising their children, we have thought how involvement in projects within the home could help meet many of these concerns. Finally, as a team we sat down and explored the facets of project work and the ways that we could show parents how they could make this approach work at home with their own children. We know that many parents have no formal training in education, but we believe that when thoroughly explained, the project approach can lead families to explore topics and engage in activities that are both meaningful and educational for children and their parents. As educators and parents, we decided to write this book on how to use the project approach and offer practical guidelines for investigation, fieldwork, use of experts, documentation, and so forth.

Just by reading this book you are taking a proactive step in providing your child with meaningful experiences that result in growth and treasured family memories. Keep in mind that some parts of the project approach might be challenging! Making time commitments for field trips and library visits, cleaning up after messy activities, and taking lots of notes as you go require extra effort from parents. While we understand the challenges (we are parents, too!), we have also reaped the benefits and joy of completing project work with our own families. We encourage you to read on with an open mind and positive attitude and learn more about the project approach.

About This Book

This book is organized into three parts. In Part I we will introduce you to the project approach and guide you in making sure that your home is a place where children can learn. In Part II we demonstrate how to introduce a topic to your child, follow through on a project, and celebrate the results so that your child feels pride and confidence in her achievements.

Also at the end of the book is a Family Project Planning Journal that can be photocopied and put in a three-ring binder to help you plan and record the project experience. The journal will also serve for you and your child as a memory book of the fun projects you have done together. We urge you to use the Family Project Planning Journal as you do your first project because it will guide you step-by-step through the process and maximize the opportunities for learning to occur. As you do more projects, you may or may not want to use the planning journal.

Part III provides information on child development and explains how to "coach" and support your child in project work and other learning experiences. We show you how to incorporate into projects meaningful practice of academic skills such as reading, writing, and mathematical and scientific thinking. In Chapter 9 we share how the project approach can be adapted for home schooling, family care, and gifted children.

Following Chapters 1–7 are illustrated stories of actual family projects so that you can see how our explanations are played out in real life. At the end of the text are a Glossary of terms used in our descriptions and Resources for Further Reading.

Whether you are a parent, grandparent, or other caregiver of a young child, we hope that our book will provide a window into the wonderful experiences that can occur when adults help make learning meaningful for children.

part I

Getting Ready for Project Work

ONE

Why Do Projects with Your Child?

You've heard about the brain research and are thinking, "Am I doing all I should be doing to help my child be as smart as she can be? Should I be playing Mozart or buying computer programs?"

Your David is having difficulty with reading and writing and doesn't seem to care. The teacher says to do more reading and writing at home, but the last thing David wants to do when he comes home is to sit and read a book!

School was a challenge for you. You don't want it to be a challenge for your child, but you don't know how to do things differently than the way you were raised.

You are beginning to feel like your child's chauffer. You take your child from sports to dance class to clubs. Dinner together is at McDonald's, and the most talking you ever do is when driving in the car.

You are a grandparent who would like to do more with your grandchild, but you don't know how you might make your time together more meaningful.

Parenting Challenges Today

No matter your income or educational background, being a parent isn't the same as it was in the past. And being a child isn't the same either. Today's schools are often competitive and dominated by tests. A wealth of new information about the brain is telling us that the experiences we provide our young children shape their intelligence. Should you be teaching your child French at age 4? Signing your child up for another class? You know too much TV isn't good for children, but what do you do *after* you turn off the TV? Is this what raising children is all about? Isn't having kids supposed to be more fun than this?

In our experiences of being parents and in working with children and families, we meet parents with questions like these all the time. We also see parents everyday who love their children and want the best for them but who may not be making the best choices about experiences for their children or spending their limited time together in the best ways.

In our work as educators and in our own parenting experiences, we have come to recognize that in-depth engagement in learning reaps enormous rewards for the growth of children's knowledge and skills. We have also found that those times when we are involved in projects with our children—when we are exploring, learning, and talking about real things of great interest to our children (both our own and those in our care)—to be immensely satisfying to us as adults.

Yet increasingly the times when children are truly engaged in learning and discovering are not occurring at all, or they are occurring when the child is with adults outside the home. For some families, learning has become something that happens at school or in a class or with "professionals." Classes, such as museum classes, can be helpful to children when there are specific skills and knowledge that they are ready and wanting to learn. However, there are many other productive ways for children, especially young children, to learn. For many parents today, the parenting role has become custodial: dress and feed them, transport them, and become their cheerleader. Although these tasks are necessary and beneficial, they are not all that parenting can be.

As parents, sharing project work with our children has enabled us to meet many parenting challenges. Through project work we have had something meaningful to talk about with our children. We have a vehicle to teach them what we value and at the same time create strong bonds between us.

What Is a Project?

A project is an in-depth investigation of a topic that is interesting to children. In families, projects are what children are "in to"—what gets them excited and what they like to talk about. Projects involve hands-on investigation, finding the answers to questions, reading about the topic (or being read to), visiting sites or places, and talking to other people (adults and children) who know something about the topic. Projects also involve documentation—collecting information and preserving the experience by writing about it, taking photographs, or videotaping.

As parents, we have experienced projects with our children. One of us, Judy, has vivid memories of the summer of the caterpillars, when her children were immersed in collecting, studying, and observing the metamorphosis of a number of caterpillars. The project involved trips to the library, studying plants and leaves, and learning about how to care for the caterpillars. (The story of the Caterpillar Project follows Chapter 3.)

Sometimes these projects become lifelong pursuits and hobbies. They become part of the family tradition. There is the "band family" whose interest in music blossomed into the whole family's involvement and support of music and probably—we don't know yet—into a career in music for a child. There is the "baseball stadium" family whose interest in stadiums turned into a project to "collect" major league stadiums by visiting them on summer vacations. In the Helm family, the girls developed a strong interest in pioneers, including pioneer clothes and toys. As they became readers this interest was fueled by the Laura Ingalls Wilder books. When a discussion began on where to go on vacation, they wanted to see the Wilder historical sites. A few years later, as the interest continued, the whole family participated in a re-creation of the Oregon Trail experience where everyone learned about the history of the West as well as how to churn butter and make pioneer crafts.

Not all projects are extensive investigations. Some projects are short-lived, lasting only a week or so. One of the joys of childhood should be the opportunity and time to explore many interests and experiment with learning about different areas of knowledge and different skills. In this way children learn what interests them and what they are good at doing. This "sampling process" provides a depth of self-understanding that enables informed selection of subjects to study in high school and eventually to career choices that promise to be satisfying. One of Judy's daughters had an intense but short-lived interest in rockets. However, her other daughter's interest in early America became a quilting project that turned into a lifelong interest, bonding grandmother and grandchild.

What Is the Project Approach?

The project approach is a method of investigating a topic by a group of children. It is an "approach" to teaching. Interest in the project approach as a teaching method has increased because the learning that occurs during projects is consistent with what we know about brain development. (We provide more information on brain research in Chapter 7.)

The project approach provides a structure for teachers to follow when guiding children's project work. About 15 years ago, Dr. Lilian Katz, from the University of Illinois, and Dr. Sylvia Chard, from the University of Alberta, developed the steps of the project approach. It is not a new way to learn. The project approach has been around for a very long time. You may have heard of other kinds of project work that teachers use such as "service learning," which involves children in community projects, or problem-based learning (often referred to as PBL). These methods are usually used with older children. In fact, PBL and case studies are used by many medical schools and especially by the Harvard School of Business.

A major characteristic of project work is the nature of children's involvement in the process. We talk about project learning as being *engaging* and *meaningful*. You can tell that learning is engaging when children are intensely interested in an experience and show enthusiasm for a project. They ask questions and discuss what they are learning, revealing a high level of knowledge for their age. Children come to project work eagerly and work long and hard. They often talk about the topic when they are not working on the project. You can see that learning is meaningful when children connect what they are learning to other facts they already know; incorporate new skills such as reading, writing, or using numbers in their study of

Amanda and Rebecca Helm became interested in pioneers before they began school. They loved dressing in pioneer clothes.

Their interest increased when they learned to read and discovered the Laura Ingalls Wilder books. They wanted to see the sites from the books on their summer vacation.

Continuing interest in "things pioneer" led to a long-term project of learning about the westward migration. The family joined a re-creation of the Oregon Trail experience.

The girls learned how to do jobs that pioneer children would do and to make toys and games. Eventually, this interest grew into a love for quilts and quilting.

As an adult, Amanda enjoys collecting antique quilts and designing quilted wall hangings. Fulfilling hobbies often begin in childhood experiences.

the topic; or indicate through questions and comments that they are doing significant thinking about the topic. Learning is not engaging or meaningful when it consists of memorization of facts without meaning or when children show little interest or enthusiasm in exploring a topic.

At times during our careers, we have been involved in gifted education; that is, providing special educational experiences to children who are considered "gifted." One thing that we have noticed is that those children who seem to be most gifted have parents who were able to identify their interests and then really support them—faning the flame of intellectual curiosity. (There are suggestions about projects with gifted children in Chapter 9.) Just as the project approach provides a structure for teachers to bring meaningful learning experiences to their classrooms, we believe that it can provide you with a structure to create such experiences in your family. As teacher trainers we have noticed that once teachers learn how to follow the structure of the project approach, they then take the techniques (such as how to help children ask questions or how to help children do observation drawing) and integrate them into the rest of their teaching. In the same way, we expect that once you know how to follow the structure of the project approach, you will branch out and use bits and pieces of the project approach throughout your interactions with your child. By doing projects with your child, you will get ideas and develop skills to support learning in a variety of ways throughout your family life.

What Happens in Project Work?

CHILDREN STUDY A TOPIC OF INTEREST

In project work children study a topic of interest for a long time. The topic comes from the children's interests. In the Helm family Caterpillar Project, for example, the children found a caterpillar in the yard and were curious about it. Their interest and questions stimulated discussion and exploration by the whole family, and soon caterpillars were a big part of their lives that summer. Even very young children develop interests and preferences.

When children are involved in a topic, they learn a great deal about it, often at a level higher than many adults would expect for their age. Sometimes children will develop knowledge and skills that surpass those of adults. We have all had the experience of being awed by the enormous amount of knowledge a child might have about something of great interest to him, such as dinosaurs or cars.

CHILDREN LEARN HOW TO ANSWER THEIR OWN QUESTIONS

In projects children learn to use a variety of ways to find answers to questions, a skill that will be very helpful in later life. The adult does not become the "teacher" of the children but a learner with the children. After children have experienced several projects, they will have many ideas about how to learn and will make their own plans with an adult's help.

Some of the ways children learn to find answers to questions include traditional resources like books and talking with "experts"—adults or sometimes older children who know a great deal about the topic. Other ways may be new to you, such as helping children do investigations on *field-site visits*. For example, a child who is very interested in cars might be taken on a trip to a car dealership where the parent and child look at many cars and compare their features. The children plan questions to ask adults and have specific tasks for the trip. Children make field notes and sketch and draw on-site. In a project on sewing, a trip was made to the fabric store to investigate fabrics.

When children come home from the field-site visit, they may want to make models, build structures, or create play environments using what they have learned. The play environments help them sort out what they are learning. For example,

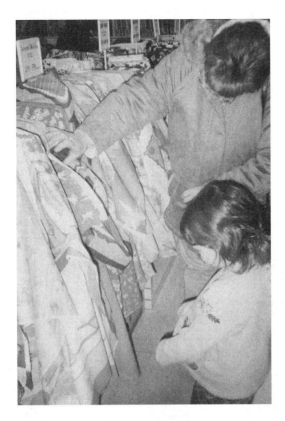

When Kaylin expressed interest in sewing, she and her mother visited the fabric store, where they looked at and compared different kinds of fabric.

the visit to the auto dealership might result in the child using blocks and toy cars to create her own dealership and garage where she can pretend to play the role of salesperson or mechanic. One of Judy's children made an apple orchard out of blocks, toy cars, and construction paper after a visit to an apple orchard.

Project work often results in a trip to the library. In the Caterpillar Project, the children checked books out of the library. They visited the caterpillar exhibit at a nature center and talked with the park ranger about how to hatch caterpillars. They also got a great deal of help from neighbors who had hatched caterpillars in the past. Notes were kept on the progress of the caterpillars, and the children made their own caterpillar book. This project provided significant motivation for the children to use "school skills," such as reading and writing, and to practice these skills in a meaningful way.

Project work can also be carried out with toddlers. They will not be able to ask questions, but an adult can observe what a toddler finds most interesting. A toddler may stop and look closely at something on a walk (such as a leaf), or carry something around (such as boxes or a ball) or become excited when she sees something (like a train).

If a toddler sees photos or pictures of trains in a book, she may point to them and use first words. These are signs of interest. The adult may then respond by

When Elizabeth showed an interest in cooking, she and her mother went to the library, where the librarian showed them books about cooking for children.

Even toddlers display preferences and interests. These toddler cousins loved balls. They collected them, carried them around, and even slept with them. Balls became a natural choice for a project topic.

providing more experiences related to the topic, such as taking the child to watch a train go by, checking train books out of the library, or providing a toy train to play with. When a large box is introduced, the toddler may pretend it is a train and want to play in it. During the pretend play, many new "train words" will be used, and the playing will show, or represent, what the toddler has learned about the topic.

CHILDREN SOLVE PROBLEMS

Another feature of project work is that children do their own problem solving, with adults helping to structure problems and assisting in finding solutions and resources. For example, in the Caterpillar Project, Judy asked the question, "What should we feed the caterpillar?" This led to the children thinking about how they could find a solution to that problem. For young children, much of the problem solving occurs as they try to "represent" their learning—through making models, building structures, or creating play environments.

CHILDREN RECORD THEIR LEARNING

Drawing and sketching are also features unique to project work. Children draw what they are seeing (even 3-year-olds draw). The purpose of drawing is not to create artists but to develop a way of looking closely at items and artifacts. When a child draws a caterpillar, he must observe very closely and notice the shapes, how parts connect, and what is different about different caterpillars. In project work, we talk about "drawing to learn." When children draw and then a few weeks later draw the same thing again, we see that the drawings reveal how much children have learned during the project. Other ways that children record their learning are project books, murals, artwork, constructions, and journals.

Toddlers are unlikely to do much drawing, although some do begin at this age. However, as in the train example above, toddlers do show their understanding through pretend play and through learning words related to the project. By listening carefully, the adult can make a list of "train words" that the toddler understands by observing the toddler's actions. For example, if the adult says, "Where is the caboose?" and the child finds the caboose, she shows that she knows the name of that train car. Another list can be made of the words that the child says. Writing down the date when a toddler appears to understand a word and the date when the toddler says the word is an easy and fun way to capture the toddler's growth in understanding.

CHILDREN COMPLETE THE PROJECT

In classrooms where the project approach is used, there is a *culminating phase* when the project comes to a close. In family projects, the topic is more likely to taper off. We feel it is important for a child to "finish off" projects so that there is a sense of closure and accomplishment and so the child can see himself as a competent learner. This helps the child develop a self-image of competence and confidence. It is a healthy way for children to develop self-esteem. For example, making a book about caterpillars summarized what the Helm children had learned about them. The book was then taken to school, shared with grandparents, and added to their bookshelf. Since a project may evolve into a lifelong interest, we encourage you to periodically make opportunities for children to stop, reflect, and share what they have learned.

How Will Project Work Benefit My Child?

YOUR CHILD WILL HAVE A REASON TO PRACTICE ACADEMIC SKILLS

Project work provides meaningful learning experiences for children; that is, it contributes to their intellectual development and has a long-term positive effect on attitudes and beliefs about learning. Project work provides a context and a reason for your child to develop academic skills such as reading, writing, using numbers, and thinking scientifically. Because your child is so interested in learning more about the topic of the project, he begins to see reading, writing, and arithmetic as valuable skills.

Reading, writing, and arithmetic are all skills that require frequent practice to perfect. Research has shown that the more children read, the better they read. The same applies to math. You may have had the experience of becoming "rusty" in using certain math skills when you haven't used them for a period of time. Although we are not saying that project work will provide all the reading, writing, and arithmetic practice that children need, especially in the primary grades, it certainly goes a long way toward providing a positive and enjoyable way to get that practice done. Project work supplies motivation for your child to sound out words, to get meaning from words in a book, or to use numbers to solve problems. Instead of the drudgery of drills and worksheets, your child practices these skills in the process of using them as tools. This is similar to the role that these skills play in our adult lives.

YOUR CHILD WILL DEVELOP DISPOSITIONS TOWARD LEARNING

Children are born with *dispositions* to be curious and deeply engaged in making the best sense they can of their experiences. One of the important features of good project work is the support of these dispositions (or attitudes) because children are encouraged to take initiative and accept responsibility for what is accomplished. We talk a lot about the development of dispositions in project work (such as a positive attitude toward reading) because we feel that they are important to lifelong attitudes toward learning and have a significant effect on children's motivation to achieve, to continue to learn, and to seek higher education.

Although you often cannot control the experiences your child has in classrooms, you can control the experiences that she has in your home. Dr. Lilian Katz maintains that young children have powerful inborn intellectual dispositions—to make sense of experience, to learn, to analyze, theorize, hypothesize, make predictions, and so forth. In the primary grades, children's experiences in school sometimes stress learning a single right answer, extensive drill and practice, and memorization. Ironically, when children reach middle school and high school, they are introduced to research and project work that requires them to analyze, theorize, and hypothesize. Teachers often struggle to reawaken these dispositions in older students.

It is these intellectual dispositions that we encourage you to support within your home, especially if this support is lacking from your child's educational experiences.

Intellectual dispositions are stronger in some children than in others. The development of dispositions is very individual. It is difficult for teachers to know the dispositions of each of the 20 or so children in her classroom. It behooves us as parents to know our children and support these vital dispositions.

YOUR CHILD WILL DEVELOP SELF-ESTEEM

Along with the development of your child's intellectual dispositions is the importance of the development of a sense of competence and self-esteem. The development of self-esteem is important to your child's success in school and in life. We all know adults who have skills and knowledge that they do not use or opportunities that they have missed in education or in their careers because they lacked self-confidence.

Many parents are concerned about their child's self-esteem because studies have shown it is related to resistance to alcohol and substance abuse, teen pregnancy, and gangs in the teen years. Yet the development of self-esteem does not come from constantly telling your child how special he is. A child quickly figures out that you are his parent and of course you think he is special. Self-esteem comes from the development of competence and resiliency, the confidence that a child has in his own skills and abilities to overcome adversity and to do well. Project work provides opportunities for your child to build that confidence.

YOUR CHILD WILL LEARN DEMOCRATIC VALUES

Children who do project work also develop a healthy appreciation for the knowledge and skills of a variety of adults and what they contribute to our society. For example, as your child learns how the car mechanic keeps people's cars running or how the grocery store manager makes sure that food is on the shelves for customers to buy, he begins to understand the concept of having a job and contributing to the welfare of others. Appreciation and understanding of the value of others is a basic understanding that your child needs to function well in a democracy.

YOUR CHILD WILL GROW IN WONDER

In addition to all the other benefits, we believe that projects can enable children to strengthen their capacity to wonder—to experience awe and appreciation—especially of our natural world. In our busy lifestyle, children are seldom given time to just sit, appreciate, and wonder about what is around them. When children's lives are constantly programmed and they are involved in activities where they primarily receive what others decide they should receive, they do not have opportunities to contemplate, to find joy in using their minds, or to think about complex topics such as life, growth, and death—the cycles of the world. As educators who have experienced many projects with children, we have continued to be inspired by the joy and the complex thoughts that children reveal when they "discover" such miracles as the emergence of a plant from a tiny seed, or an egg hatching, or a machine that comes to life and moves. In project work, your child can have experiences that will connect her to her world and the people in it in more meaningful ways than just learning knowledge or developing skills. Although as educators we tend to talk about benefits of project work as growth in knowledge and skills, as parents we want to also emphasize what we have observed in our own children—the development of a heightened awareness, a connectedness to the world, almost a child spirituality that becomes a foundation of resilience as our children mature and face some of life's major challenges.

How Will Project Work Benefit Me as a Parent?

YOU WILL MAKE TIME FOR YOUR CHILD

One problem with our increasingly technological world and our busy lives is the decrease in meaningful parent-child time. In some families, having parent-child time together almost has to be scheduled—like making a date with someone. When you and your child are doing projects together, there is immediacy to the time spent together. If your children are raising caterpillars, then going to the nature center to learn what to feed them isn't something that you can put on a "to do someday" list where it will never get done. The need for project information and project support requires that you make time for these experiences to occur, and in the process of making time for project work, you (and your child) are making time for each other.

YOU WILL DISCOVER A PARTNER IN LEARNING

Another benefit of project work is the joy of watching your child learn what you value and what you think is important. With the narrowing of curriculum and the increasing emphasis on testing and tests scores, many beneficial experiences for children are neglected or eliminated from school, such as art, music, and physical education. You cannot depend on experiences your child has in school to develop a rich background in these areas.

If you want your child to value music, then you need to explore music with him. As you encourage and support your child's interest, you can also open up your own interests to him. When your child shows interest in the baseball game you are watching and asks a question, you can answer the question and then return to the game, or you can take time to introduce him to other concepts about the game. If that interest continues, you might decide to approach learning about baseball as a project for the two of you to do together.

The project approach can serve as a structure for passing on interests and values rather than letting them grow by happenstance. Both you and your child will enjoy the activity, and you may discover in your child a friend with whom you will now have a lifelong-shared interest—perhaps a baseball buddy.

If you have limited knowledge about a topic, you may be surprised to find that your child brings a new perspective to it. Experiencing a project, such as learning about turtles, can be intellectually stimulating to you. It can provide a break from thinking about the day-to-day demands of your job or the responsibilities of caring for a family. For example, when a child visited an airport and saw an airplane, she noticed a little hole in the plane and asked about it. This discovery led to an explanation of the ventilation system of the plane, which was information new to the adults as well.

Especially interesting are field-site visits, which often result in looking "behind the scenes" at familiar places such as stores, zoos, or garages. Even these familiar places become more interesting when seen through the fresh eyes of a child. An explanation of how the scanner works at the grocery checkout (of course, this explanation is requested only at nonbusy times) might result in peeking behind the counter and examining the equipment. This can be interesting for adults as well as children. Many common parent and child activities, such as going to see a children's movie or playing games at the pizza place, are frankly boring to parents. One reason is that they are designed only for fun, and we quickly tire of their entertainment value. Our mind wanders back to the problems of everyday life. However, you will find that learning new things captures your mind, especially if you are concentrating on helping your child get his questions answered, thinking of thoughtful questions that you can ask, or trying to remember information so you can discuss it with your child later. The intense concentration is like exercise for the brain, and as with physical exercise, you will feel refreshed and less stressed after you do it.

Engaged interest and curiosity is not just good for children's brains; it is good for adult brains, too. There is truth to the saying that children keep you young. "Use it or lose it" is certainly true for adult brains. As parents, and especially grandparents, you can be intellectually stimulated by the task of supporting your child's interest through project work. If you also have your own questions about the topic, then you model lifelong curiosity for your child.

As part of project work, you will learn from talking with people from a variety of lifestyles. Conversations with adults from different occupations can provide you with the same appreciation and understanding of others and the contributions that they make to our well-being that it does for your child.

YOU WILL STRENGTHEN FAMILY RELATIONSHIPS

To us as parents, the biggest benefit of doing projects with our children is what it does for family relationships. As you work together with your child, you will discover her strengths and talents. A common comment from the parents we have introduced to project work is that they have learned so much more about their children. Parents talked about their child's approaches to learning, their sense of humor, and the surprising depth of knowledge and skills that were revealed. Several parents said that they came to appreciate their child as a separate person with interests, likes, and dislikes. Most talked about feeling more connected and closer to their child.

Are projects the answer to everything? No, of course not. Children also need many other experiences, including help with homework and some access to experts through classes or clubs. However, we feel that projects can greatly enrich family life and build a bond between you and your child that will smooth the bumps of his growth to independence. The project approach provides a structure for making that happen. In this book we will show you how to guide and support project work in your home. We will take you step-by-step through the project process.

In the next chapter we will explain how to arrange your home environment to support project work. But first we invite you to read about the Swenor family project—a study of their own dog, Maude.

MAUDE THE DOG PROJECT

PHASE ONE

Sometimes finding a topic takes looking right under your nose! As the Swenor family thought about interests that might have project potential, topics such as dinosaurs and bridges came to mind. As parents, Mimi and Joel knew that neither of these topics would provide hands-on opportunities and active, engaged learning. Thinking closer to home, the family, which included 3-year-old Gordon and 2-year-old Evan, decided to study their family pet, Maude the dog. The family began messing around with the topic by reading books about dogs, listing questions about Maude, building a Lego model of Maude, and finally, constructing a topic web together.

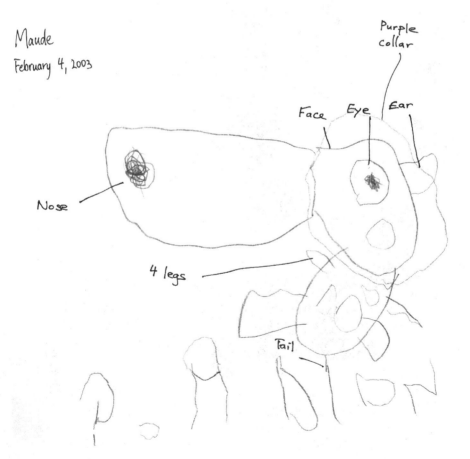

Three-year-old Gordon made this sketch of Maude. His mother labeled the parts as Gordon told her what to write.

PHASE TWO

During this phase the family took Maude to the vet for a checkup and investigated all the questions on Gordon's list. He graphed the numbers of body parts (eyes, ears, legs) Maude had, sketched Maude on the examining table and labeled her body parts, observed the taking of blood, and assisted the vet in weighing Maude.

Upon return home, Gordon and his family began a construction of Maude out of papier-mâché. As this activity continued, Gordon was also involved in experimenting with dog treats for Maude and recorded which ones she liked best. Gordon also got his friends at school involved by taking a survey of which families owned a dog. He put the results of his survey questions on 3 x 5" cards that fit in each child's mailbox and collected the data. Gordon had the idea to organize a birthday party for Maude and invited some of his friends from preschool to enjoy an afternoon of "pin the tail on the dog," running with Maude, and eating birthday cake.

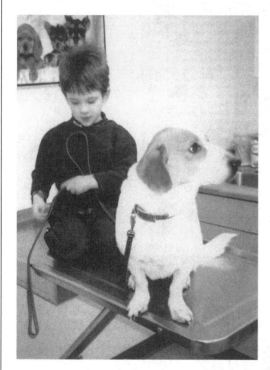

Gordon is really getting into the vet visit! He had many of his questions answered by the veterinarian.

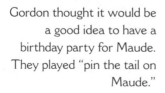

Gordon thought it would be a good idea to have a birthday party for Maude. They played "pin the tail on Maude."

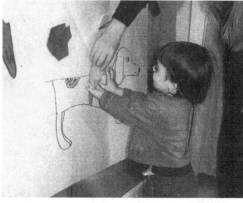

PHASE THREE

To celebrate the culmination of the project, the Swenors brought Maude to Gordon and Evan's school, and the boys presented all the new information they had discovered about Maude. Many children asked Gordon questions about Maude, and he quite enjoyed his 15 minutes of being the expert.

The final celebration was when Joel, Evan and Gordon's father, brought Maude to visit the children's classrooms. The other children had many questions for Gordon.

Making Your Home a Place for Learning

To focus on a project, your child must feel "safe" to dig into materials and really explore with his work. It is not necessary to make major changes in your household to make it a place where meaningful learning experiences can occur for your child, but there are questions for you to consider.

1. **How can I provide an environment for learning?**
   Where is there enough space in my home for my child and me to work together? Will I be comfortable working on a 12-inch wooden chair alongside my child? Where will my child have a surface to write, draw, paint, and use materials like clay?

2. **Where will I get materials for my child to use?**
   Will buying supplies for project work be expensive? What kinds of things do I need to collect? Will I need to go somewhere special to get the materials we will use?

3. **How can I store materials for projects and other forms of meaningful learning?**
   Where will I keep paper, clay, and books about project topics? Where can ongoing work be stored so that it is safe from siblings, vacuum cleaners, or the dog? Where can materials be stored neatly and safely, but so that they are still accessible to my child?

4. **How I can I help my child gain literacy skills in project work?**
   Are there things I can do to encourage my child to use books more? What kinds of books would be appropriate for project work? How can I best organize literacy materials?

5. **How can I provide the time for projects and other forms of meaningful learning?**
   When can we block off time so we can concentrate on our project work? Can we fit clay work in between a soccer game and girl scouts?

In this chapter we will help you answer these questions.

Creating an Environment for Meaningful Learning

As an adult you have learned that you need space to do quality work, whether it is your kitchen, your office, or a workshop. Children also need space to do quality work. With patience, determination, and a little creativity, most living areas can accommodate project work. If you think in advance about issues such as table space or access to water, you can help prevent many problems that may come up once your child is busy with his project. For example, your child will not have to stop work early so you can clean off the table for dinner.

For some parents, creating an environment for meaningful learning can be a challenge because it requires them to leave their comfort zone. In our role as teachers and parent educators, we have come across parents who say,

> "Give my 3-year-old scissors? Is that safe?"
> "Bring paint into my immaculate kitchen? Do you know what we spent on that floor?"
> "I can't let my child use these things when I have a toddler in the house too!"

Issues of stains, safety, and appropriateness all emerge. One advantage of doing project work with young children is that it encourages you as a parent to think about the organization of your home. Does your home foster meaningful learning for your children? If you work out how to create spaces for meaningful learning in project work, you can use these for years to come as children work on school projects and other learning activities.

While creating a space may seem difficult on a tight budget or in a small home, just the willingness to create a space and provide materials will benefit your child. Neither a fancy art studio nor 100 different types of collage materials are necessary for a child to be able to do project work. If money or space is an issue for you, think creatively of how you can assemble an inexpensive art kit of basic supplies (scissors, glue, crayons, paper), which will be enough to get your child started. Using found materials such as shoe boxes, wrapping paper, and buttons can also be a way for children to develop their creativity. Keep in mind that many great project activities have occurred using just a few materials on the kitchen floor or at the dining room table covered with newspaper.

When looking at your environment for a space where you and your child will want to work together on projects, you will need to consider the room, its location in the home, and the furnishings within that room.

FINDING A LOCATION IN YOUR HOME

Survey your home. Is there a playroom, a kitchen breakfast bar, or a dining room table that may be a good place to work? The room where you work should be a place where you will be able to access materials easily. Good work spaces for children are not necessarily fancy. A heated garage room or a finished (or even unfinished) basement room may be perfect, as long as it is comfortable for you and your child when you work on larger projects. A quieter, less busy place without a television playing allows for more communication and concentration during activities. The room where you and your child work should be free from a constant stream of traffic and allow a child to feel that her work is safe, especially if there are other children in the family. Toddlers and friendly dogs can be especially dangerous around art supplies, so a less-visited room may be helpful. Since one of the goals of doing projects with children is to provide meaningful time together, this time with your child is precious. The environment must support your focusing on your child and the interaction between you and your child.

SELECTING A WORK SURFACE

While a small table and chairs in your child's room may be perfect for a tea party, a 6-foot, 220-pound father will not be comfortable in this pint-sized area! Likewise, a 3-year-old seated on an adult folding chair at a table that is chin high for the child will not help the creative process. An appropriate sized table—large enough for lots of materials and chairs—is important. Kitchen counters are great if there are stools and there is space. However, a dining room table or kitchen table may work better.

The table or counter area needs to be washable and able to handle markers, clay, and paint. Using a vinyl tablecloth may help make a dining room table or a counter area appropriate for projects. Having a washable floor underneath is also helpful. Kitchen linoleum is fairly durable and washable, but if the most comfortable area to work side by side is carpeted, old blankets, sheets, newspapers, or drop cloths can be placed under the work table for protection.

In small apartments or in homes where there is limited space, it will probably work better to have work surfaces and materials that can be put away when not being used. For example, a large piece of cardboard can be used as a place to work and can be slid under a bed when not in use. Some families have set aside one corner of a room as the children's work area and put materials in this area.

CONSIDER ACCESS TO WATER

Project work can also occur in several different places. At some times, access to water is crucial, such as during art and construction work. Activities such as painting or clay work require water. It may be possible to carry water to the work area, but for cleaning up accessible running water is important. Imagine your child finishing a big painting project—do you want to have him walk through the house with hands dripping with paint? Of course, paper towels and baby wipes can provide a quick fix, but access to a sink is preferable.

Collecting Materials for Project Work

To do project work, your child will need certain basic art and writing materials. Keep in mind that you need not go out and buy all these items immediately, but

Jenny covered the kitchen floor with newspapers to provide plenty of space for her three boys to spread out and use the crayons and markers for drawing.

By covering the dining room table with a vinyl tablecloth, Nannette was able to safely paint her map and not worry about keeping the table clean.

you can add to your collection gradually and as needed. You may discover some of the items in your house now by just checking cabinets and closets.

Ask yourself the following questions and notice the possible answers we suggest. Our list of materials should help you figure out what you already have and what you need to get:

1. What will we write and draw with?
   Markers
   Chalk
   Crayons
   Pens
   Pencils
2. What will we write and draw on?
   Paper
   Chalkboard
   Old envelopes
   Note cards
3. What will we paint with?
   Sponges
   Brushes
4. What will we use to hold things together?
   Glue
   Tape
   Tacky glue
   Staples
   Brads
5. What will we cut with?
   Child scissors
   Adult scissors
6. What will we use to sculpt?
   Clay
   Wire
   Play Dough
7. What will we use to clean up our mess?
   Paper towels
   Sponges
   Baby wipes

These questions will help you organize what you will need before you get deep into project work and construction.

When shopping for project supplies, you should check out dollar stores and discount stores, which often have inexpensive markers, paper, and paint. To reduce costs, you can use scrap paper. Envelopes, junk mail, notes, or letters may be blank on the back and can be used for drawing and painting. Paper can be recycled paper. Many of the best materials for constructing and making models are junk materials. Grandmas, aunts, and neighbors can help search for materials. Often things considered trash to others (for example, "packing peanuts," cardboard, bottle caps, colored cellophane, or foil wrap) can be treasures to a family involved in project work.

Storing Materials for Easy Accessibility

Storage is an issue in most homes with children. Toys, shoes, and jackets abound, sometimes appropriately on shelves and in closets and other times spread throughout the house. Storage of materials for project work (and artwork in general) takes a little planning, but when well organized, it can lead to many hours of creativity and development of many skills beyond project work.

As a parent, you need to emphasize that materials must be kept neatly organized so they will be available for use. Art materials should be valued and seen as something very special that deserves special care. Materials such as scissors, markers, and glue can be seen as dangerous items in the home, but when used properly and with respect they offer children many opportunities to express themselves and support meaningful learning. This is especially important for preschoolers. As educators, we have often observed how disadvantaged children are who came into kindergarten and primary grades without extensive experience with scissors, pencils, and markers. The more organized these materials can be, the more interest your child will show in using them. There is something very appealing about markers standing in a mug, can, or cup ready for use and paper sorted by color like a rainbow. Artwork is usually a meaningful learning experience, even without being part of a project. It requires children to focus, to take initiative, and to think creatively.

Depending on your home and the room you have selected for project work, storage options may be an issue or may be taken care of by the room itself. If you are lucky enough to be working in a room with a closet or pantry, you may be able to allocate a shelf or two to the storage of materials.

On each shelf plastic shoe boxes or school pencil boxes can help keep materials neatly organized. Wooden baskets are definitely more attractive, but they may be costly and do not allow a child to see what is in them. You can also use cardboard boxes that you pick up at a grocery store. (Your child may want to decorate these with markers or paint.) Photocopying stores and office supply stores often discard boxes designed for paper that have sturdy lids.

You may also find that you have a storage or display item that can be easily adapted. In the Helm family, the plant container on an old wicker plant stand provided space for paints, brushes, clay, markers, rulers, and other equipment. Shelves were added below the plant container to hold paper. This "art center" was used first in a family room, moved to the kitchen in the next house, and then moved to the basement work area as the children grew and their projects required more work space.

If you do not have the luxury of built-in space, rolling plastic file drawers may be helpful. Found at office supply stores, these rolling carts may have three of four

The art shelf is located in the kitchen pantry at the Berg house. When the pantry doors are closed, materials are hidden.

The Berg's pantry has many uses. Shelves are designated for kitchen appliances, art materials, adult "office" supplies, and Rubbermaid boxes of toys.

The Berg's art shelf is labeled and organized for the children. Though young, the children are able to independently access materials with a step stool.

Sometimes more space in the home allows for a storage cabinet and shelves. Pegs in the wall create additional storage space for bags of fabric collage materials.

drawers to store paper, markers, and other materials. These can be easily moved and "hidden" when necessary. Cardboard boxes can also be piled one on top of the other to function like a cart with drawers.

Whichever system you choose, your child needs to understand how to put his materials away when he is done. If your child can read, labels with words ("glue," "markers") will do the job, but a younger child may also need a picture or drawing to go with the words. While labeling might seem time consuming, after your child uses the materials she will be much more likely to put them away in labeled containers. When it is time to use them again, she will also be more motivated when she sees the materials neatly arranged rather than haphazardly thrown into a drawer. For bigger or more bulky items such as those used for collage and construction, one large Rubbermaid storage box will work fine. When found items such as bottle caps or packing materials are easily accessible, searching for the perfect material adds to the creativity of the project.

Creating a Literacy-Rich Environment

An important outcome of project work is the involvement of your child in literacy (reading and writing). As we pointed out in Chapter 1, in good project work your child learns how books and reading materials can help them satisfy their curiosity. They will also learn the value of writing. Setting up your home to encourage reading and writing is a first step in this process. Most of us make sure our children have many books. Those books usually have their own storage place—a shelf, bookcase, or plastic bin. With just a little more time and effort, you can create a literacy-rich home environment by incorporating some of the following ideas:

- Make sure the space you have selected for project work has a flat surface for writing and drawing and that there is enough room to lay out reference books as your child is writing and drawing.
- Start a collection of different kinds of writing tools like pens, pencils, fine-line markers, and colored pencils and store them neatly in a cup. Also see the list of materials above.
- Collect different kinds and sizes of writing paper for writing, making signs, and labeling (long strips are great for labeling and note cards work well for signs).
- Keep a picture dictionary with the writing supplies. "Pictionaries" help children spell frequently used words. Some examples are
  — *Best Word Book Ever* (R. Scarry, 1999, New York: Random House)
  — *Richard Scarry's Best Picture Dictionary* (R. Scarry, 1998, New York: Random House)
  — *Scholastic First Dictionary* (J. S. Levey, New York: Scholastic)
- Store or display the books used for reference during project work near the writing supplies. A small plastic tub works well for this.

COLLECT REFERENCE BOOKS

Involving your child in collecting reference books is very important and encourages her to think about what she wants to learn. Going to the local library for books is always a good experience for families, whether project work is involved or not. With the Internet so accessible and the creation of book superstores (such as Borders and Barnes & Noble), we often forget about what a wonderful resource libraries can be. The librarian can serve as an expert as she guides you and your child to the appropriate section and recommends certain books.

As you are selecting reference books, make sure to think about the illustrations. Real photographs are much better reference tools than an illustrator's drawings. Realistic diagrams about how things work are also especially helpful. Children want to see *real* information, and it's much easier to learn about the physical characteristics of birds, for example, if you have photographs to look at.

Consider using adult books or books for older children, not for your child to read, but for the wonderful and detailed photographs. These books are often expensive, and unlike pictionaries or storybooks, they are unlikely to be reread after the project ends. It is more practical to check them out of the library than to limit your child's access to books to what you can afford to purchase. When using books that are more advanced, you can paraphrase the words and make the information meaningful for your child. Remember that the whole purpose of the library visit is to find books that will support your child's explorations.

After the books have been collected, store them near the writing materials in the project area. This way they will always be close to the work at hand, which will encourage their use as reference materials. When you hear a question like, "Do birds have ears?" you can reply, "Gee, I'm not sure. Let's look it up in the bird book from the library." When there is an exchange like this between you and your child, you have modeled a process for finding answers to a question, and your child has taken a first step toward becoming an independent learner.

USE THE INTERNET

Another excellent literacy tool is a computer with access to the Internet. Although preschoolers and very young children cannot search for information on the Internet, children can view pictures that a parent finds and read (or be read to) articles that are printed from Internet sources. There are excellent sites that provide information on many common project topics.

However, it is not necessary to have a computer in your home to use the resources that are available on the Internet. Internet access is available at public libraries, and if you do not know how to use the Internet to search for information, a librarian can usually help.

It is important that you do not immediately use the Internet to answer all of your child's questions or to overload your child with information. Children need to find information on their own and to experience the joy of discovering information. Young children (through primary school) learn best through firsthand

The resource materials used for the Slime Project included a mixture of fiction and nonfiction books.

experiences: touching, manipulating, looking at something from many angles, playing with things, and closely examining real objects. This does not happen through the computer. When the computer is used as the main way to learn, the child who has not yet mastered reading and writing must depend on an adult to do the work. This places the child in a passive role in the learning experience and will not result in your child developing independence and self-confidence, which are part of project work. However, the Internet can provide access to wonderful photos, diagrams, and drawings that you can print out and add to the other literacy materials that your child uses.

Finding Time for Project Work

Perhaps the biggest challenge to doing project work is finding the time. With a variety of family dynamics (two working parents, single parents, and children with special needs), finding time for project work may seem next to impossible. Sporting events, music lessons, birthday parties, and dentist appointments overflow the calendar, and just getting everyone bathed and to bed may seem like a major accomplishment for the day.

Whether or not you can find the time for project work may be a matter of the importance you place on your child's development of the knowledge, skills, and dispositions we discussed in Chapter 1 and the level of commitment that you are willing to make so that projects happen. Do you want to contribute to the academic development of your child? Is this project something that is important to you and your child? Do you want your child to cherish memories of the two of you work-

ing together? If you answered "yes" to the above questions, then you can probably find time for project work.

It is also helpful to think creatively about your use of time. Is it possible to
make project plans as you unload the dishwasher or run errands? Is there a part
of the project your child can be working on as you cook dinner? Try to brainstorm
when these activities can best fit into your family's daily routine and schedule.

REDUCE TV TIME

Think seriously about the time your child spends in front of the television. The
American Academy of Pediatrics warns against television for children under the age
of 2. Guidelines recommend no more than one hour a day for preschoolers and no
more than two hours a day for children in primary school.

Are we as families somehow able to work watching television into our busy
day? Television is one of the biggest distractions to spending quality time with our
children. Many of us have gotten into the habit of having the television on constantly for entertainment or even for "background" noise. It is true that clicking
on the television is much easier than helping your child paint. However, encouraging your child to try a second draft of a drawing or getting out library books on
your project topic require about the same amount of time.

When it comes to really focusing on your child, turning off the television does
a number of things. First, it cuts down on stimulation and noise that interfere with
you and your child's concentration. Second, television can easily steal the attention that you and your child are giving to your special activity. Finally, shutting off
the television says to your child, "You and our time together are my priority." This
message will go a long way toward helping your child feel valued and supported
as a learner.

DEVELOP A FAMILY SCHEDULE

It is important to think realistically about where project work might fit into your
family schedule. Project work can be adapted to a variety of family structures. Some
families may want to plan exactly when to do project work. Others may know that
a large block of time on a certain day of the week is regularly available. For example, in the Berg family, Monday and Wednesday nights are usually free and everyone is home for supper and activities together afterward. For the Bergs, weekends
are very busy and might only allow for a few "pick-up" activities. In the Scranton
family, weeknights are "hairy," but Friday evenings are devoted to family activities,
which allows for an uninterrupted evening of quality time. Other families may find
that combining project work with other family activities and family jobs works well
for them.

Most importantly, think about how the learning that comes from project work
can fit into your family and make a habit of taking time to learn together. Project
activities must be comfortable for all involved so they provide an enjoyable experience and are continued. Of course, short activities such as reading books or

researching on the Internet may occur at any time, but it is nice to designate a time for major project work sessions. Spending quality time with children is really about commitment. As you make time for project work, remember what priceless family connections you are making—an investment that you will not regret.

Documenting Project Work

As you prepare to begin project work in your home, one additional consideration you need to keep in mind is *documentation*. In the project approach, *documentation* describes the process of collecting and keeping evidence of your child's work and the learning that is taking place. Documentation includes things like written notes, photographs, actual work from your child, and reflections from your child. These items are saved and later can be used in creating scrapbooks or other displays of the project. In Chapter 6 you will learn how to use documentation to celebrate your child's learning. In your collection of materials, several items are helpful to assist you in documentation but are not required, such as folders to put things in and something to take notes on such as a spiral notebook or Post-it notes. Cameras and video cameras are good additions to help document project work if you have them, but they are not necessary for good project work to take place.

On pages 10 and 11 of the Family Project Planning Journal at the end of this book, you will find a checklist that will help you look at your home and get ready for project work. Remember, however, you can begin a project at any time and then build your project materials and work areas as the project develops. Reading the following story about the Slime Project can help you.

SLIME PROJECT

One of the families who made the most of their home environment was the Schellenberg family, who completed the Slime Project. Jenny (the mom) supported her boys' learning as she allowed them to store worms in the refrigerator, measure worms on the front porch, and create a final celebration display in the dining room. The Schellenberg house is a typical home and did not have a special place for project work to occur. Through some of the ways suggested in Chapter 2, Jenny was able to create space and arrange materials for project work. Using creativity and organization, Jenny was able to help the boys research the answers to their questions and engage in hands-on, meaningful learning.

As an art experience, Joshua painted with slime. Using a different medium allows for a unique painting experience.

PHASE ONE

As a mother of three boys under the age of 5, Jenny thought long and hard about what kind of project would work for her family. The two older boys, Joshua, age 3, and Caleb, age 4, enjoyed playing with flashlights and making shadows, but she felt the topic was limited and perhaps not "hands-on" enough to keep her sons engaged. As she thought about what the boys really enjoyed, "slime" came to mind. The children enjoyed the sensory experience as they played with this wetter, slicker form of classic Play Dough.

Working with the idea of slime, Jenny began to think of slimy items that would be more concrete and readily available for her boys to explore. As she remembered Caleb's interest in worms that appeared as they had dug up bushes the previous summer and in a slug they had found in their sandbox, Jenny thought that slimy types of creatures just might be the topic for them. The boys also enjoyed a video called "Bible Man" with a superhero who could turn bad guys into slime. To get the boys focused, Jenny went to the library to get a variety of books about creatures such as snails and worms.

In order to study and observe slimy creatures, Joshua and Caleb added new pets to an aquarium. Caleb labeled the aquarium, *Snail.*

P H A S E   T W O

After making a web of what they knew and wanted to learn, the family took a field trip to Presley's Worm Ranch and to Super Pets. On their visits the boys made field sketches of newts and snakes and brought home a box of worms to study. Jenny took many photographs of creatures they were observing. During their Phase Two work, Jenny and the boys made a variety of slime recipes, drew with crayons and markers, and worked with clay. The boys created many clay models of slugs and snails they had observed. As they studied the 26 "pets" they had brought home from the worm ranch, the boys measured, compared, and labeled as they learned about their worm friends.

We counted _26_
worms in the box.
Then we measured how
long they were. Some were

To develop math skills, Caleb used a ruler to measure their worms. He recorded their length on a chart made by his mom.

_4_ in., _5_ in., _6_ in., _7_ in.,
_8_ in., and _12_ in. long.

To culminate the project, the family displayed their work—posters, drawings, photographs, and sculptures—in their dining room and invited their extended family to visit. During the visit the children provided tours and served "Dirt Dessert" (chocolate pudding with crushed cookies and gummy worms) to their guests.

About the project Jenny reflected:

Overall it was a learning experience for us all. Caleb loved drawing and painting, and it was a good time to encourage writing. He began to think of questions and seemed to enjoy learning about the animals. Even though he's shy and not a go-getter type of learner, I saw growth in him, and once we were done, he was satisfied. I really liked working with my kids on the project, and I know in the future there will be many topics to explore. It takes planning, thinking ahead, and being in tune with my kids' interests. Documenting took time, but it was worth it and was fun to share and celebrate all the things we did and learned. It seemed somewhat different to do a project at home than in the classroom, but it reinforced that learning about things the children are interested in is important and builds their confidence as active learners.

Caleb's Worm Ranch Experience

"We went to the worm farm. We saw them in the refridgerator. He put them in a box. He dumped them out. He told us to keep them in the refridgerator at home. We took them home. We played with them. We counted them. They felt slimy. They were not all the same size. Some were small and some were big. We put them in the fridge."

Caleb reflected on his own work and learning during the Slime Project. Jenny recorded what he said.

part II

Carrying Out a Project

THREE

Overview of the Project Approach

If you have not had an opportunity to observe project work or have not experienced project work as a child, you may feel at a loss as to how to get a project started with your child and then follow it through. The project approach—an "approach" to project work—provides structure for planning and supporting projects with children. There are three phases in a project: Phase One, getting started with a topic; Phase Two, investigating that topic; and Phase Three, celebrating the project and the learning that occurred. In this chapter, we will give you an overview of the three phases of project work. Then each phase will be described in more detail in subsequent chapters. The project approach flowchart shown on the next page in this chapter provides an overview of what happens in each phase.

Phase One: Getting Started

Phase One of a project begins when you notice that your child shows interest in something. It may come about from something the child finds, discovers, or just happens to see. Or you may create an interest by introducing something to your child. This "something" is called a "topic." Identification of the topic of the project is the main event in Phase One. During this time, you and your child narrow the topic, becoming more specific about what your child wants to find out. For example, an interest in trucks may become a project topic of pickup trucks. An interest in fishing may become a project about tying flies. During this phase, you make a list, or web, of what your child knows about the topic. (How to make a web is explained in Chapter 4.)

Next, you help your child form some questions. What does he want to know about this topic? During the project, your child will find the answers to these questions. Phase One ends when both of you have agreed on questions for investigation.

The Project Approach for Families

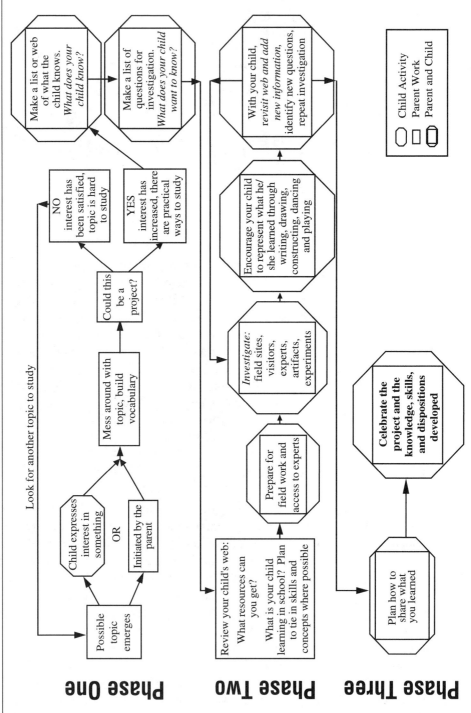

Phase One

Possible topic emerges

Child expresses interest in something

OR

Initiated by the parent

Look for another topic to study

Mess around with topic, build vocabulary.

Could this be a project?

NO interest has been satisfied, topic is hard to study

YES interest has increased, there are practical ways to study

Make a list or web of what the child knows. *What does your child know?*

Make a list of questions for investigation. *What does your child want to know?*

Phase Two

Review your child's web: What resources can you get? What is your child learning in school? Plan to tie in skills and concepts where possible

Prepare for field work and access to experts

Investigate: field sites, visitors, experts, artifacts, experiments

Encourage your child to represent what he/she learned through writing, drawing, constructing, dancing and playing

With your child, *revisit web and add new information,* identify new questions, repeat investigation

Phase Three

Plan how to share what you learned

Celebrate the project and the knowledge, skills, and dispositions developed

Child Activity — Parent Work — Parent and Child

40

Phase Two: Investigating

Phase Two is when the investigation of the project topic takes place. The main feature of this phase is your child's in-depth study of the topic—efforts to seek answers to the questions listed in Phase One and to identify new questions. During the first part of Phase Two, you will do some preparations for the investigating. As we mentioned in Chapter 1, an important part of investigating is visiting what we call a *field site*. Once you select a field site related to your topic, you should find out in advance what experts might be there and make arrangements for your visit before you go. Before your visit, discuss with the experts and employees at the field site what your child is investigating and the specific questions that your child is asking. A trip to the library during Phase Two will result in books for you and your child to share. New vocabulary is learned in a meaningful way, and your child will notice that books are a good way to satisfy his curiosity.

Phase Two is also a time when your child will make and build things related to the topic. Phase Two is a wonderful learning experience for your child because he will develop skills such as asking questions, using construction tools such as staplers and tape, and taking notes (either by drawing or writing, depending on his age). Your child will likely come up with more questions to be answered. Phase Two may last for several weeks or several months.

During your child's investigation, you will want to document the process. You will take photographs, write notes, and collect your child's drawings and written work. This documentation enables both you and your child to see and appreciate her growth in knowledge, skills, and dispositions. Your child will see that she is a competent, successful learner.

When your child begins to lose interest in the topic and seems to be more involved with other activities and events, then it is time to end the project and celebrate the learning. There comes a time in the life of every project when children are ready to move on to other things. This can happen for several reasons. Children may simply no longer have questions; their curiosity may be satisfied. Children may also have reached a point at which further investigation requires skills, such as reading and writing, beyond their current abilities. The topic of the project and the previous experiences of the children can also affect the length of the project. The project may simply have run its course.

If you are new to projects, you may think that the waning interest indicates that the topic was wrong and that the project failed. You may feel disappointed as your child loses interest and turns to other topics. However, any topic can be run into the ground! Waning interest is part of the natural progress of a project and indicates that it is time to move into Phase Three.

Phase Three: Celebrating Learning

For children the main task in Phase Three is to decide what and how to share what they have learned. Your role includes talking with your child about what she has

Four-year-old Elizabeth and her mother made this web when they began a project on cooking. A task of Phase One is recording what children know and want to know about the topic. Elizabeth wanted to know how to make recipes.

During Phase Two children do lots of hands-on investigating. Here Elizabeth is learning about eggs and how to separate the yolk from the white.

During Phase Two, Elizabeth's parents found her in the kitchen writing measurements on recipe cards. She wrote 4 and copied the word "noodle" from a package of noodles.

During Phase Three, children and parents celebrate the learning and mark the end of the project in some way. Elizabeth made a thunder cake and served it to the family. She was proud of her creation.

learned, reviewing the project by looking at the work and photos you have collected, and helping your child recognize what she has learned. This time of celebration is important because during this process your child's self-image as a learner can be strengthened. This is also a good time to talk about how it feels for your child to satisfy his intellectual curiosity and to have pride in his accomplishments.

Summing Up the Project Approach

We think you might find it helpful if we summarize the main events of the three project phases in the following list:

PHASE ONE: GETTING STARTED

> Observe your child's interest or create an interest
> Mess around with the topic
> Consult books and other materials
> Write down what is known about the topic
> Make a list of questions for investigation

PHASE TWO: INVESTIGATING

> Investigate and find the answers to questions
> Visit places, go to the library, look on the Internet
> Help your child represent what he is learning (drawing, writing, building)
> Record what is happening with photos and notes
> Ask more questions, find more answers
> Recognize when interest is waning

PHASE THREE: CELEBRATING LEARNING

> Celebrate the project
> Help your child decide how to share what she has learned
> Discuss your child's accomplishment with her

Elizabeth's project on cooking illustrates the project phases. See how these events on the next two pages represent events in the phases summary above.

Another guide to doing projects at home is the project approach flowchart shown on page 40. You will likely want to refer to it again and again.

There is also a copy of the flowchart in the Family Project Planning Journal. On the flowchart you can see the three phases of project work and the way each phase progresses. The information in the shapes within each phase will serve as a reminder of the activities and experiences that can occur. If you follow the flowchart, opportunities for maximizing the learning that occurs and the development of your child's knowledge, skills, and dispositions are more likely to occur.

Now that you know more about the structure of the project approach, we thought you might like to read more about the Caterpillar Project that occurred in the Helm family and was mentioned in Chapter 1. As you read the story about the project, which follows this chapter, you might see how the activities of the project are similar to what might naturally happen in many families who are supportive of children's learning. The difference in making your support of your children's learning into a "project" by applying the project approach is that opportunities for learning are extended and learning is made more visible to the parents and the children (and therefore more likely to occur). By following a structure, a parent is reminded to think about ways to enhance the child's learning. These ways might include writing down a list of questions (which supports reading and writing skills), helping children make models (which builds spatial relationships), taking time to celebrate what children have learned (which enhances the child's self-image), or focusing family experiences on what the child finds interesting (which supports and develops curiosity and interest in learning).

It is important to remember, however, that the project approach provides a structure but not a prescription for learning experiences. There is a fine line between supporting your child's investigation and learning and taking over the learning experience. One of the most challenging tasks in raising young children is learning how to recognize that line and avoid crossing it. If you take over the project, it is just another time when your child does not experience self-initiated learning and curiosity. Those wonderful dispositions to investigate, to discover, and to find answers will not be strengthened. The structure of the project approach can help you support rather than crush your child's curiosity and natural dispositions to learn while achieving learning goals.

As you think about the project approach, keep in mind the definition of the word *approach:* "a way or means of reaching something," "an entry" (*American Heritage Dictionary*). The project approach can be an entry, a way to reach your goal of supporting your child in active, engaged, meaningful learning and intellectual development. As an approach, it is important to remember that an entryway is never the end destination. The structure of the project approach is a guide for you to support your child's learning, but it is not an end result.

Following the story of the Caterpillar Project, Chapter 4 guides you on what to do in Phase One.

CATERPILLAR PROJECT

When the Helm girls, Amanda and Rebecca, were 8 and 4 years old they discovered a caterpillar in their backyard. They came into the kitchen to get a container so they could keep the caterpillar under control and observe it without hurting it. Their mother, Judy, found an empty peanut butter jar. In the wicker art center in the kitchen, where paper, pencils, paints, and other equipment were readily available for investigations, she found the magnifying glass and handed it to Rebecca. Amanda put the caterpillar into the jar and placed it in

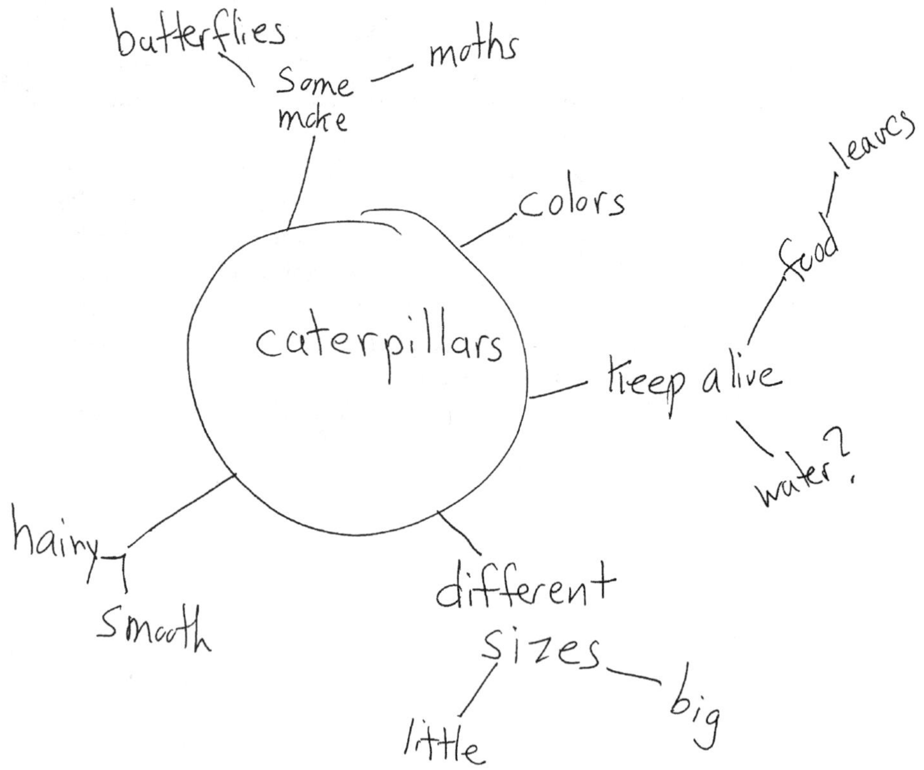

butterflies
Some — moths
more

colors
leaves
food

caterpillars

keep alive
water?

hairy
Smooth

different
sizes — big
little

Observations and beginning knowledge about caterpillars was recorded by Judy from the girls' comments.

the center of the kitchen table. As the girls looked carefully at the caterpillar, Judy put papers and pencils on the table to invite observational drawing.

As the children were drawing the caterpillar and talking about it, Judy observed them and tried to figure out what they did and did not know about caterpillars. Amanda knew that caterpillars turned into butterflies. She also knew that the caterpillars for each butterfly looked different. She told Rebecca what she knew. The children watched the caterpillar for some time and then went on to do other things. The drawings were placed on the refrigerator.

Later, Judy looked in their children's encyclopedia about caterpillars. When the children came in from playing outside, she showed them the article about caterpillars and helped Amanda read the article to Rebecca. When they finished reading, Judy asked them what they knew about caterpillars, and she made a web, which was also placed on the refrigerator. One thing they had learned was that each kind of caterpillar eats certain leaves. The children recognized that they needed to identify the caterpillar they had found so that they would know what to feed it. If they didn't, it would be difficult for them to observe the caterpillar through its complete life cycle.

PHASE TWO

A trip to the library was planned. Judy helped them write down some questions that they needed to find the answers to. These included

- What kind of caterpillar was it?
- What would it turn into?
- Can we keep the caterpillar and watch it turn into a butterfly, or will it die in the jar?
- What does this caterpillar eat?
- Does it need water?

When they got to the library, they asked the children's librarian about books on caterpillars and shared their questions with her. She suggested several different books, which they checked out. One had information on their caterpillar, which they discovered would turn into a moth, not a butterfly. Rebecca and Amanda then wanted to know what the difference was between a moth and a butterfly, which led to more reading.

The librarian suggested that they may want to go to the Forest Park Nature Center where she had seen a display on caterpillars. She said that the ranger there was very knowledgeable about caterpillars. When Judy and the girls returned home and while the children were playing, Judy called the Nature Center and shared the children's interest. She found out what might be available at the center for the children and when a ranger would be there to talk to them.

Museums, nature centers, and parks are good places to find answers to project questions. Forest Park Nature Center had a caterpillar display.

Rangers and museum personnel are especially helpful when they are alerted to children's interests and questions. The girls found information on their specific caterpillar.

On Saturday, Amanda and Rebecca went to the Nature Center with their father, Richard. They took their list of questions and the book about caterpillars containing a picture of their caterpillar. There was indeed a wonderful display, and the ranger looked at the book, answered the girls' questions, and suggested how they could keep the caterpillar and watch it change.

When they got home, Richard helped the girls construct a cage, and they collected the leaves that the caterpillar would need to eat. For the next several months, more caterpillars were collected with the girls carefully observing what plants the caterpillars were on or near. They made several more trips to the Nature Center for more questions and advice. Notes were taken on a calendar. Judy suggested that they keep a list on the refrigerator for new questions and photograph the caterpillars. Several caterpillars completed the growth process, turned into moths, and were released.

PHASE THREE

As the last moth was released, Judy suggested that Amanda and Rebecca make a book that told about their caterpillars and gave them a scrapbook in which they could paste their drawings and photos. She encouraged the children to write captions for the drawings and pictures. The scrapbook was taken to show Grandma and Grandpa on their next visit, shared with a number of friends, and taken to school in the fall.

FOUR

Phase One: Getting Started

Now that we've presented an overview of the three phases of a project in Chapter 3, we can focus in separate chapters on each phase in more detail. Let's get started with Phase One!

The most important events in Phase One are selection of the project topic, introducing it to your child, and helping him think of the questions that will be the essence of his investigation. For young children (toddlers through about third grade) the selection of a topic to investigate contributes substantially to the quality of the work children will do. Very young children have had fewer experiences upon which to draw and have a limited knowledge base and a limited vocabulary. In general, you will find it helpful to spend time and effort exploring a topic and encouraging your child's interest and curiosity in the topic before you decide if it will be suitable for a project.

Identifying Your Child's Interests

Topics are most likely to be received enthusiastically by young children when they are already among their interests. A good place to start is to just observe your child and see what he is interested in. Your child may spontaneously express interest in a particular object (such as a backhoe being used for road repairs), an event (such as grandma going into the hospital), a particular place (a nearby restaurant such as Pizza Hut), or a story or book about a topic. Your child may show this interest by asking questions or requesting more information on the topic.

With a younger child who has limited verbal skills and little vocabulary related to a topic, you can look for expressions of interest through her behavior, perhaps by observing her spontaneous play. For example, a 3-year-old may push forward for a closer view of something that interests her. She may often pick up particular items or hoard "souvenirs" of experiences such as items collected on a walk. Very young children also signal interest by spending more time focusing on particular objects or listening to conversations more attentively than usual. If your child, even though very young, is interested in a topic, he may attend closely to what you and other children are saying and try to be part of the conversation.

These young children were taking a spring walk when they became fascinated by moss growing on rocks. Often chance encounters with something new and different result in project topics.

School-age children enjoy touching, feeling, and even taking apart objects to learn about them. The more objects children can interact with, the more likely the project will keep children's interest.

Selecting Project Topics

Even with extensive experience of implementing project work, we are often surprised by how young children respond to a topic: some that we expect to work well fail to engage them, and others we are skeptical about seem to take off.

CHILD-INITIATED TOPICS

Children often start their own projects. Sometimes the topic emerges out of an event that provokes a child's curiosity. You may notice that suddenly something happens and your child becomes immersed in a topic and raises many questions for investigation. For example, building and construction commonly become the focus of a project when construction of a building begins near your house and your child observes it while coming to and from other activities. One characteristic of a project that is child initiated is that it often moves into the investigation phase quicker because it isn't necessary to spend a lot of time encouraging interest or building background information. The Caterpillar Project that you read about in Chapter 3 was child initiated.

PARENT-INITIATED TOPICS

Not all projects will begin with your child. You may choose a topic because it seems to provide beneficial experiences. For example, you may initiate a project about hospitals because your child will have to go to the hospital in the future for a medical procedure and you think it would be good for him to have some knowledge about the place before he goes.

On the other hand, you may initiate a topic because you are aware of opportunities for your child to learn about a subject. An example from projects done in classrooms is the Real Estate Project, which took place in Judy Cagle's multiage classroom. She initiated an investigation of the topic of houses when she discovered that a subdivision was under construction across from the school. She realized that the young children would have an opportunity to observe the development of the subdivision from the first digging to the actual sale of the houses over the entire school year. As the project developed, she listened and watched for the young investigators' expressions of interest as they progressed into the first phase of the project. You can initiate topics in the same way.

There are many advantages to broadening your child's knowledge and experiences by reading nonfiction books, visiting interesting places, watching educational TV programs such as a program on animals, and simply bringing interesting things into the home. Not all experiences you provide for your children are directly tied to project work. When you take time to expose your child to a wealth of experiences and accompany that exposure with words and explanations on the child's level of understanding, you open up the possibility for meaningful interests to develop.

Often familiar sites, such as the shoe store, become the focus of project work. When looking for project topics, you might want to visit familiar places and observe what interests your child.

Here is an example from the Helm family. While walking with the girls one day, Grandpa Harris came to an area where a new sidewalk was being built. The earth was flattened, and there was a hole with string guides and forms for the sidewalk. Grandpa Harris stopped and directed the children's attention to the process, pointing out how the concrete rests on the dirt and how the form and string keep the edges of the sidewalk straight. Grandpa initiated a conversation with a worker nearby, asking several questions. In this way, Grandpa modeled intellectual curiosity and interest while also introducing words that the children may not have known.

This building of background knowledge and modeling of intellectual curiosity can contribute to your long-term goal of intellectual development for your child even when it does not result in a project. When these kinds of experiences become routine in your family, your child will find many opportunities to develop interests. Some of these interests may result in project work, which will further enhance your child's intellectual development. There are additional ideas of ways that you can interest a child in a topic in the Family Project Planning Journal at the end of this book.

GENERAL GUIDELINES FOR SELECTING A TOPIC.

Although it is clear that topics of interest to your child should be the main focus of a project, it is also important to note that not all a child's interests are equally worthy of the kind of time and effort involved in good project work. There are differences in topics—some are great for talking about or for reading a book about, but when sustained interest is desired, some topics are better than others. Here are some guidelines to help you choose good project topics:

1. *A good project topic includes real objects. Children enjoy touching, moving, and using real objects in their play.* Children learn by touching, moving, carrying, modeling, hearing, tasting, and looking closely. Choose a project topic that has many real things that are safe to handle, not just ideas. For example, fire trucks is a better project than fire fighting; mirrors is a better topic than reflections.

2. *A good project topic is connected to something your child knows about.* Children like to learn about things they already know something about. It is hard for young children to think about topics for which they have little experience or words. Boats might be a good topic if your child has been in a real boat but not so good if he has never seen a boat. Think about your child's daily life. What does he see? Where does she go? What is around your neighborhood? For example, the ocean is not a good topic if you live in the middle of the United States.

3. *A good project topic can be investigated at a place you can visit, preferably again and again.* Children, especially young children, benefit from seeing real places. If a child can only learn about something from books or photos, he may develop unrealistic ideas. For example, studying the ocean without ever visiting it might result in a number of misunderstandings. Think broadly about places to visit. A field-site visit might be a short walk to your garage, to a store at the end of your street, or to your neighbor's garden. Your child will also benefit by going to places again and again. When you first take your child to the zoo, he may have difficulty focusing on just the monkeys, but after a visit or two the rest of the zoo won't be so distracting. When you choose a topic for project work, think about where you might visit. Learning how your lawnmower works might be a better topic than studying airplanes, which requires a trip to an airport far away, because you can easily go to see a real lawnmower and you can do it over and over again.

4. *A good project topic can be researched by your child.* Research for young children consists of observing, manipulating, experimenting, asking questions, trying out ideas, and visiting places. Young children are less interested when they have to listen or learn only through books, videos, encyclopedias, or what an adult tells them. Your child will learn more when she can "study" a topic herself (touch, poke, turn, etc.). Projects work best if you can be a resource and help your child rather than a lecturer on the topic.

5. *A good project topic enables your child to use skills and methods appropriate for his age.* Children like to share what they know through drawings, paintings, sculptures, or playing. Young children especially like to make play places, such as a McDonald's restaurant, where they can pretend. Is there something that your child could draw, paint, make a model of, or use for pretend play?

6. *A good project topic is worth studying.* Projects take time and effort, so what children study should be worth learning about. For example, learning the characters in

a favorite video may be interesting, but it won't help develop school skills or engagement in school subjects. It would be better to learn how a car works or what happens in a grocery store than to do a project on a movie character. This is especially true if your child has little interest in school.

7. *A good project topic is related to your child's world.* Projects should help children learn about their daily world and their family and community. The world of young children is very small—family, neighborhood, and school or care center. Projects that are based on family interests are especially meaningful. For example, if there is a family tradition of fishing and many adults in your family fish, this could be a great project for you and your child. If your family loves to make their own pizza, learning about pizza parlors and how they make large quantities of pizza might interest all family members.

Messing Around with a Topic

It is important when doing projects with young children to take time to build a background of knowledge about the topic. We call this "messing around with the topic." It is not question focused but just a time when you learn some things and build a vocabulary so that questions can emerge. You can mess around with the topic in several ways to build a background and to enrich discussions before investigation begins. For example, Grandpa Harris, after walking with his granddaughters and seeing the sidewalk construction, returned home and found a diagram in a how-to manual that showed how a sidewalk was made. He also told Grandma Harris about their discovery and encouraged the children to talk about what they had seen. The next day he talked with the construction workers putting in the sidewalk and arranged to have the grandchildren there when the pouring of cement began. He was providing an opportunity for his grandchildren to mess around with the topic of sidewalks.

Another way to introduce a topic is to tell a story of your own experiences and ask for stories from your child. For example, if you think dogs might be a good project, you might tell about a dog you saw and ask your child to tell you about a dog he saw. You might also share an artifact, such as a piece of familiar equipment, to provoke curiosity and discussion. A picture book can be read and discussed. Conversations about the topic can be encouraged. For example, you might tell the children any questions that you have about the topic or what is especially interesting to you about the topic.

Because young children can represent their experience and understanding through their spontaneous play, you can also begin a project with young children by introducing props or costumes and showing your child how to play with them. For example, you might create an apron and a toy cooking area for your child who appears to be interested in cooking. As he plays, he will show what he understands related to the topic. Young children may also draw or paint what they know about a topic or build a block structure. This process will build a shared perspective, a sense of togetherness about the topic between you and your child, and the joy of exploring something of interest together.

With school-age children, messing around with the topic often includes reading a book together, making an exploratory site visit, or even watching a video. Making models or diagrams are also a way to build vocabulary and develop interest.

Finding Out What Your Child Knows

The more you talk about a topic with your child, the more you will know what your child might have questions about. This will give you ideas of whom to talk to and where you might like to visit. There are several ways that you can document or record what your child knows. You can

> Make a web
> Make a list of questions
> Save drawings
> Photograph things he builds
> Write down what she says

MAKE A WEB

Webs are graphic representations that are especially helpful for understanding and illustrating relationships between things. Webs are similar to lists except that the items are represented as radiating from a central idea.

Sometimes adults new to projects are hesitant to use webs because they feel that young children cannot read words and do not understand the relationships represented by the connecting lines. However, experienced project teachers report that children as young as 3 seem to understand and respond to webs more readily than to lists. The process of having their words written on a web appears to be understandable to many 3-year-olds. Adding drawings or photos to the web assists the youngest children in connecting the written representation with their words and the words of other children. Many 4-year-olds are actually able to explain the relationships between words as they are connected on the web and are also often able to recognize the words. For children who are in kindergarten or the primary grades, webbing is also a wonderful way to refine vocabulary. This helps with their reading comprehension.

Notice the web from Ashley's Horse Project above (the story of this project follows Chapter 6). Ashley's mother asked her what she knew about horses and then wrote down her answers. Sometimes it is helpful to bring up specific aspects of a topic, such as "what about taking care of horses, what do you think they might do to take care of horses?" Ashley's mother did not type the web on the computer until later when she made a book about the project. During the process of webbing, words are usually written by hand. However, if you have access to a computer and technology, you can certainly enjoy using it for documentation of project work, and webs are a good place to do that.

In Phase One you, just as Ashley's mother did, can create a web to record what your child knows about the topic as you are introducing and exploring it with him.

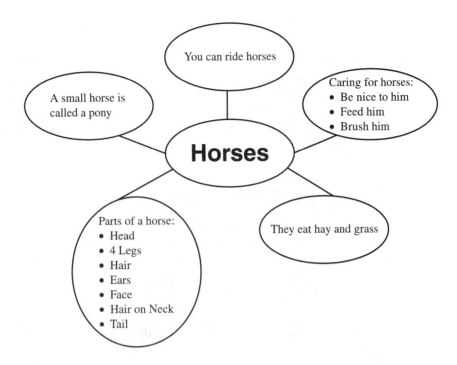

Questions about horses:

1. What are baby horses called?
2. What are daddy/big horses called?
3. Where do horses live?
4. What else do horses eat?
5. How do we care for horses?
6. Is it a mommy or daddy horse?
7. Do they poop standing up or sitting down?
8. When can we ride a horse?

Ashley's mother recorded what Ashley knew about horses in a hand-drawn web. Later, she put the web into a computer program, printed it out, and put it up for the children to see.

LIST QUESTIONS FOR INVESTIGATION

As you mess around with a topic with your child, you will notice if she is maintaining interest or if interest is beginning to wane. Often young children will be interested in a topic for a short period of time. They will get their questions answered and then will move on to other topics. This was a good learning experience for your child but will not be the focus of a project. Look around for a new topic.

If your child continues to be interested and has questions he wants to find answers to, then you are ready to write questions down and move into the investigation phase of the project. You may want to write the questions in a list on a question web. Young children will often have only one or two questions. Don't be surprised by this.

Very young children (toddlers and young 3-year-olds) may not even be able to formulate a question. That is ok. Don't be discouraged. Often when the child is at a field site or working with objects related to the topic, more questions will spontaneously emerge. You can add these to your list as you go along. Once you have a list of questions, you can move into Phase Two of the project, which we talk about in Chapter 5. But first we encourage you to read about the Race Car Project.

How do we make brownies without a recipe?

How do you make cookies without a recipe?

How do you make applecrisp w/o a recipe?

Why does dad smash the potatoes when he makes mashed potatoes?

How do you make sugar?

Elizabeth had many questions about cooking. However, most of her questions focused on recipes and food preparation. Recipes and cooking skills became the focus of the project.

RACE CAR PROJECT

PHASE ONE

Christina is the mother of Joshua, age 4. Joshua showed an interest in race cars very early. Racing is a popular activity in West Liberty, Iowa. He liked to play with toy cars and began taking them apart and putting them back together at age 2. This interest increased when he began playing a computer game that had a car race as the main feature of the game. He also became very interested in seeing the races on ESPN and quickly learned the names of some of the drivers and their cars.

Christina thought race cars would be a good topic for a project, but she decided to ask Joshua what he would like to study. She suggested several other topics, including dinosaurs, which she knew that Joshua also liked, but as she predicted, race cars was his favorite and became the project that they did together.

Christina spent time with Joshua specifically devoted to their project. She listened as he told her what he knew about race cars, what he liked about them, and what he would want to learn about them. Christina quickly became aware that Joshua already knew a lot about race cars, more in some cases than she knew.

Joshua made a painting and a drawing of a race car. Joshua told Christina that he had written the word *gas* on his drawing.

Joshua used tempera paints to make this painting of a race car.

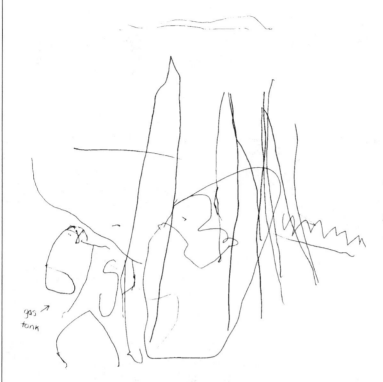

In this first drawing of a race car, using a marker, Joshua has written a *G* and an *S* for the word *gas* where he thinks the gas tank is located.

gas → tank

PHASE TWO

Together Christina and Joshua read books about race cars and looked up information about different kinds of race cars. Christina remembered that she had a friend, Matt, who had a car that he raced locally, and she called him and asked if she and Joshua could visit. She then asked Joshua for his questions before they visited Matt. This is the list of Joshua's questions and Matt's answers.

1. How do they build the engine of a race car?
   Answer: A mechanic builds it.
2. Do you put oil in your car while you are in the pit?
   Answer: Not in the pit.
3. How much gas do you put in your car before the race?
   Answer: We don't use gas; it runs on an alcohol fuel cell. It takes 22 gallons.
4. What is your number?
   Answer: 18.
5. Do you use a jack to look under your car?
   Answer: Yes.

Christina also added her own question, "How fast does the average car go?" They visited Matt and saw the racing car, which Joshua got to sit in and pretend he was driving. Christina described the visit in this way:

The day that Joshua was able to visit a race car driver was exciting. He sat in the seat and pretended to drive the car.

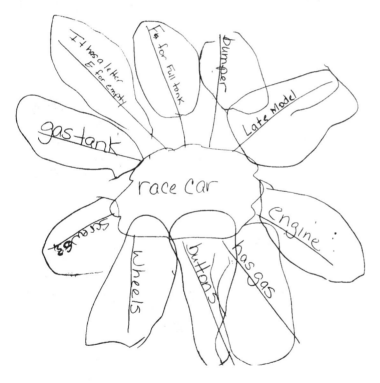

It was a letter E for empty

$ for Full tank

bumper

Late Model

gas tank

race car

engine

scrapes

wheels

buttons

has gas

Christina recorded what Joshua had learned about race cars after they did their field-site visit. Webbing is an excellent way to see what words and concepts your child remembers.

He was so excited—his eyes were lit up, "Can I please go in it?" He right away pretended to drive and made noises—telling me all about it and where the engine was and how fast he could go.

Then Joshua asked Matt his questions, and Christina wrote down the answers for him. Joshua remembered all of the questions himself and did not need to be prompted. This surprised Christina, who thought this indicated

Near the end of the project Joshua used markers to make this drawing of a race car. When you look at Joshua's first and second drawings (Time 1/Time 2) side by side, you can see how much more Joshua understands about real race cars.

how strong his interest was in the topic. Matt also taught Joshua the correct names of the types of cars in the local races.

When they returned home, Christina had Joshua tell her what he had learned about race cars, and she recorded it in a web. She also got out some paper and markers, and Joshua drew pictures of race cars. She was pleased at how his pictures looked so much more like race cars than his earlier painting and drawings did. He also did some writing.

P H A S E   T H R E E

Christina and Joshua worked together to make a poster about their project. On the poster were pictures of Joshua driving the car, his first painting of what he remembered about a race car, and two of his marker drawings of a race car. Christina also put the questions and their answers and the web on the poster. They also included the names of the cars that Joshua had learned. Christina wrote them down exactly as Joshua told her to.

late model—it is the fastest car
modify—it is the second fastest car
pro-stock—it is the third fastest car
bombers

Joshua traced the letters for the title of the poster. Joshua took the poster to school for sharing, and then Christina put it up at home.

Joshua continues to be interested in race cars. Christina asked him if he wanted to do a project on something else, and he said, "No, I still want to do the project on race cars." Christina is thinking about how they might continue the project by building model cars or visiting other places. Joshua's older sister Jasmina, age 11, now wants to do a project, and Christina is beginning a project with her on trees and plants.

About the project with Joshua, Christina says:

What I got out of it was seeing his interest and talking with him about it. It was a bonding time for us, to hear him talk about it and to just listen was such a joy. To see him excited about it, seeing him wanting to get up in the morning, and say "Lets do it." It is making me try to even get other interests out in him. I see now that you can build on those interests that a child has, and it can be really educational in a fun way. It brought us closer together and gave us something good to do. I've passed on to other parents to try this.

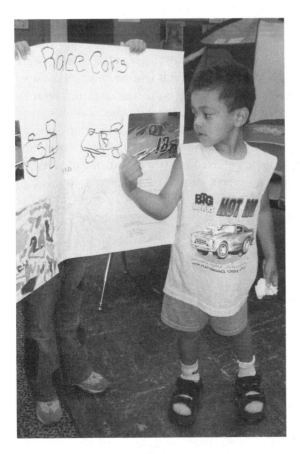

Christina and Joshua collected their work from the Race Car Project and made a poster. Joshua traced the words *race cars*. Posters are a simple yet effective way to celebrate a project.

FIVE

Phase Two: Investigating

After you and your child have developed a list of questions on your project topic, you are ready to enter the most extensive and rewarding part of project work—exploring and investigating. In Phase Two you will select and visit field sites, choose experts to consult, seek answers and record results, draw, paint, construct, and of course, play! Phase Two is the longest and the most active phase and probably the most meaningful part of the project for your child. During this time, you will get much information about how and what your child is learning, and there will be many documentation opportunities. Your photographs, collections of your child's work, and observations will enhance your understanding of what your child is learning and how to be responsive to him. As classroom teachers, we often find this part of project work to be the most exciting, when we can watch and record the learning taking place! You can observe your child's approach to solving problems and help your child become a confident problem solver during play/project work. You can also encourage your child to become a reader and writer.

Visiting Places

After your family has decided on a topic to explore, one of the first decisions to make is where to go in your community to find answers to the questions under investigation. A visit to a place for the purpose of investigation in project work is called a *field-site visit*. These field-site visits are extremely important to project work because they provide answers to many of your child's initial questions—what your child is wondering about the most. For example, during the Helm family Caterpillar Project, it was important to go to the Forest Park Nature Museum, where many different caterpillars could be studied and observed in their natural habitat. Talking to the naturalist at the park gave the Helm children many opportunities to ask their burning questions. Recording the answers either through their writing or drawing helped them become responsible for bringing the information home to be organized.

On a field-site visit children are encouraged to explore and look closely at equipment and materials. Photographs and drawings help children remember what they did and saw on the visit.

You and your child can plan a field-site visit together. The following planning activities will make the visit more productive:

- Prior to your visit, talk to the person in charge at the field site to make sure your visit will be a "hands-on" experience for your family.
- Prepare a list of questions to ask the person in charge or an expert during your visit.
- Gather a few clipboards, paper, and pencils for drawing and writing.
- Take a camera or a camcorder, if possible, to record important aspects of the visit. (Looking at photos or a video at home helps your child remember what she has seen.)
- Allow enough time during the visit for sketching and listing things observed. (Make sure your expert knows ahead of time that you'll be drawing with clipboards and taking pictures.)
- Allow enough time for playing, if appropriate. (For example, during a visit to a machine shed, the children were given time to climb on and sit in the tractors.) Planning time for dramatic play encourages your child to represent his learning in a different way.

If there are younger siblings in the home, especially babies, think about getting a sitter for the field-site visit. Focusing on the children who are involved in the project work will reduce frustration for the whole family. Very young children don't care about sketching a pizza oven and would likely keep you from supporting your child who is interested. Other adult family members, like grandparents, can feel a part of the family project by caring for those younger members of the family.

When the field-site visit has been successful and your family finds new information and has new experiences, chances are good the entire project will be a success. It is worth taking time to plan and carefully prepare for this part of project work. The field-site visit will set the tone for what happens next!

On page 13 of the Family Project Planning Journal, there are some ideas for preparing and participating in a field-site visit with your child.

Talking with Experts

Finding an expert to answer your child's questions and encourage learning is another important task in planning for Phase Two. When one thinks of experts in any field of study, one usually thinks of very educated, professional people, but that is not always the case in project work. When your family is investigating a topic like pizza, the pizza maker at your local Pizza Hut becomes the expert for this project. When you are exploring cars and car engines, you will want to find a mechanic who will answer your child's questions patiently and support your child's investigations by letting him manipulate some engines and tools. A project expert could be your next-door neighbor who happens to know a lot about gardening and would be willing to let you and your child explore her garden. It could be a relative, like a grandpa who has an extensive coin collection and would be excited about helping his grandchild learn about different coins during a money project. Or the expert could be someone who works at the field site and is willing to help deepen your child's understanding of the project topic. Think outside the box. Who would know the most about your family's project topic? Who knows? You may end up much closer to that neighbor, relative, or employee!

Things to consider when you are choosing an expert include

- Is she willing to devote some time to your project? This could be one hour, or it could be several visits over several weeks.
- Will he be open to the idea that your child will need to be actively engaged in the exploration, such as touching or manipulating real objects connected with the project topic?
- Will she be flexible? Could the expert come to your house, or would it be more convenient to go where she is?
- Will he have any resources that he would be willing to share, for example, books, maps, posters, photographs, real objects, or tools?
- Can she recommend possible field sites to visit?

On page 14 of the Family Project Planning Journal, there is a checklist for selecting and communicating with an expert.

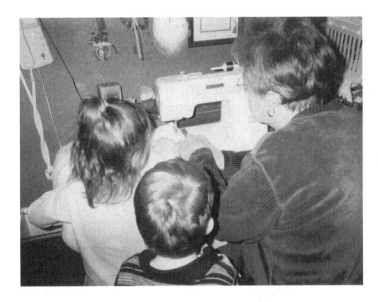

Kaylin and her grandma are experimenting with the different parts of the sewing machine as they work on Kaylin's Sewing Project.

Representing Learning

When children are actively involved in meaningful learning, they have many different ways, or many different languages, to tell us about their learning. These different languages include talking, drawing, building, playing, making up songs, and making up dances, among others. These are all ways that children can represent what they know. As teachers, we often talk about the results of these experiences as *representations*. If a child draws a bridge, we say that the child is representing his understanding of the bridge through his drawing. The picture he creates is called a *representation*. An important component of Phase Two is representation. It is through representation that your child can sort out what she has learned about a topic and connect it with other information she already knows and understands.

An important aspect of the representation process is documentation. When representation is occurring, you will probably want to take photos of the process and not just collect the finished product. For example, photographs of how your child built a large block structure to represent a building he studied would provide much more information than just a photo of the finished product. Taking notes of what your child says during the process will also provide insight into what each block represents to her.

When you, the parent and colearner, take time to document what is happening as your child is engaged in representing, you are creating a window into her thinking. Your own understanding of your child is deepened and strengthened by the documentation. In the following sections of this chapter, we will give ideas for documenting your child's project work and discuss the different ways to support your child as she is learning.

OBSERVATION DRAWING

One benefit of project work is the strengthening of children's observational skills. As we mentioned in Chapter 1, the best way to encourage this skill is through drawing. When your child draws what he is seeing and then later comes back to that same drawing and redraws it, he is able to show you in the language of his drawing what he has learned about that topic. Drawing during a field-site visit is also a way for your child to take notes about what he is seeing. In our project work in the classroom, it is common to have children as young as 3 do observation drawing.

Although many adults think of drawing as a talent, it is actually a skill that can be supported in children. If your child says to you that she can't read, you would likely tell her that she will learn to read. It will take some work and practice, but reading will be something that she will learn to do. Your child then approaches the task with confidence. If you react to your child's comments or concerns about drawing in the same way, she will approach drawing with the same confidence and will develop a skill that will be valuable throughout her life.

Beginning to Draw

It is helpful to teach your child how to do observation drawing before your first field-site visit. To begin your first drawing session with your child, find something in which your child has expressed interest, attach some paper to a clipboard, find some sharp pencils or fine-line felt markers, and then sit by the object with your child.

Drew is concentrating as he sketches the different parts of a shoe during a field visit to a local shoe store.

You should also be engaged in the drawing process and might have to model some problem-solving techniques. For example, your child might say, "I can't draw that bridge. It's way too big, and it's got way too much stuff on it." Break the drawing process down by modeling on your own paper and by thinking out loud. You might say, "I think if I start with those big beams I can get the shape. Look, there are ten big beams, so I should draw ten big beams on my paper." In Chapter 8 we explain more about guiding your child in drawing.

As your child finishes his sketch, ask him about it and help him label the different parts of the sketch to encourage literacy. Come back to the sketch later, and ask your child to think about how he would change it. This is a technique called "redrawing," or "Time 1/Time 2 drawings." It is an effective way for both you and your child to see what he is learning from the project experience. Remember Joshua's race car drawings. Ask your child to reflect on what he changed in the second drawing and why. Document—write down—his responses, and add this information to the project journal. Encouraging children to think about their own learning strengthens dispositions to work hard and to evaluate one's work. Encouraging these dispositions will result in your child becoming a lifelong learner.

Collecting Equipment for Drawing

It is not necessary to have elaborate materials for teaching your child how to use drawing as an observational tool. As we noted earlier, you will want to have the following materials available whenever you do project work or go on a field-site visit:

> Clipboards
> Plain white paper
> Sharp pencils or fine-line felt markers

A clipboard is a necessity because it provides your child with a firm surface for drawing and writing wherever you happen to be exploring. An inexpensive clipboard can be a piece of cardboard from a box with a paper clip or hair clip to hold the paper on the board. Tying the pencil to a string and attaching the string to the clipboard avoids the frustration of losing the pencil. With very young children (3 and under), we have found that fine-line markers are better for drawing because children that young often don't have the muscle control to make a strong mark on paper with a pencil. Black works best.

DRAMATIC PLAY

After children take a field trip or visit with an expert, they will come home wanting to represent what they have learned. One way they do this is to engage in dramatic play. How many times has your child played house and assigned roles to others ("Okay, I'm the mommy, and you be the daddy")? Or come home from school only to become the teacher and "teach his students"? If you observe your child in this pretend play, you will see what she knows about family structure and how her

Time 1

Time 2

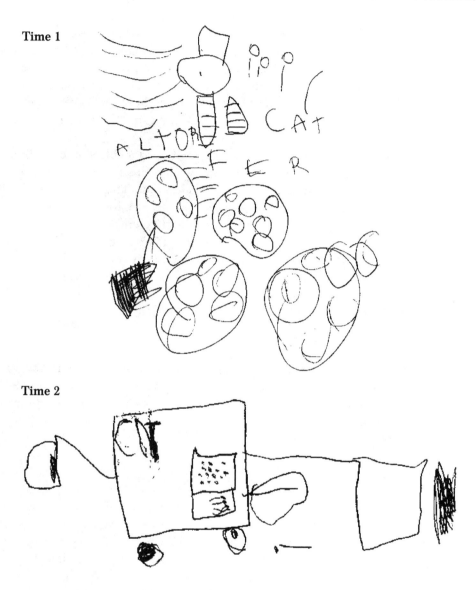

Collecting children's drawings at the beginning and the end of a project captures their growth in understanding from project work. These are Elizabeth's Time 1 / Time 2 drawings from a project on construction machines.

classroom works. Similarly, when you take a trip to the grocery store and your child comes home and wants to be a cashier, he is telling you what he knows about how a grocery store works.

Recognizing the Importance of Dramatic Play

Dramatic play is also a form of symbolic thought. When a young child is pretending that a block is a box of groceries that he puts on the truck, he is using the block as a symbol of the groceries. Children's ability to think symbolically is similar to the kind of thinking that occurs in reading comprehension. Children create pictures in their minds as they play; that wooden truck on the rug is a big truck going down the highway. This is the kind of thinking that will enable them to create pictures in their minds when reading words on a page. In addition to practice in the use of symbolism, in dramatic play the child is also using new vocabulary as he plays a role and learning about sequence and story plot. These all contribute to reading comprehension.

Encouraging Dramatic Play

As a parent, you can support your child's dramatic play by preparing your home environment. You can encourage your child to represent what she is learning about the project topic by creating what we call a *play environment*. You can do this by

- Involving your child in collecting needed props for play about the topic (aprons for a bakery, an old keyboard for an office, etc.)
- Designating a place where the dramatic play props can be accessible for several days to encourage persistence and continuity
- Incorporating some literacy activities when appropriate (such as making menus for a restaurant or painting a sign for a bakery)
- Participating in the dramatic play, if asked, and helping your child organize the play into real sequences by asking questions ("Should I wait in the waiting room if I am the patient?")

As the play continues, your child will often want to incorporate other forms of representation into her dramatic play. For example, if she is playing in her construction of a doctor's office, she may at some point bring in doctor's exam tools that you and your child have made with found materials. Alternatively, if you and your child are building an airplane out of a large box, the two of you might want to construct control panels and levers to help your "plane" fly. These play environments may not always look like "models" to you. However, if you listen to your child's conversation and see that he is using a bottle cap as if it were a button on the control panel, or he grasps the straw he haphazardly stuck on the box as if it were a lever, you will see that in his mind it does represent the real object.

Keeping handy a bin of found materials encourages dramatic play. Often objects that look like trash to adults are treasures in the hands of a child. Things to save and store include the following:

These children are playing in the dentist office that they constructed during a project.

Paper towel and toilet paper tubes
Styrofoam meat trays
Bottle caps
Empty film canisters
Small plastic containers
Cardboard pieces in good condition
"Packing peanuts"
Yarn and string
Bolts and screws
Sculpting wire
Corks

One way to support your child's dramatic play following a field-site visit is to help her remember details about the real things she saw. Looking at photographs taken during the visit or reference books with good photos will inspire your child to remember specifics as she is constructing. A good technique for you as a parent to enrich dramatic play is to review the photos with your child and ask if there is anything in the photos she would like to add to the play environment.

MODELS AND CONSTRUCTIONS

One of the most exciting ways children tell us what they are learning is by building and constructing models of what they have been investigating. In the Scranton family, after an autumn trip to the apple orchard, the children decided to make an orchard with blocks and toy trucks. As children understand more about the topic they are studying, a natural extension is for them to build a model of it. For young children—preschool through kindergarten—most models begin with some kind of blocks. If you do not have blocks, use discarded pieces of wood. As your child constructs the basic form, bring out the junk bin with materials he can use to add details to his model. Incorporate literacy into the construction by suggesting that he label streets, buildings, or important landmarks. For example, if he is building a model of the zoo you visited, he could label each cage with the type of animal in it and make signs showing directions to each area.

Practicing Math and Science Skills

As your child is busy constructing, she is also using many important math skills. When she is trying to figure out how long to make her sign for the restaurant, she might use a ruler to measure the length. Or when he is making a control panel for his tractor, he might need to count out how many buttons he will need. During a garden project, your family might need to sort seeds a certain way, giving your child the opportunity to practice classifying skills. Becoming aware of these math opportunities (we will talk more about this in Chapter 8) will help you organize your project work for that day and allow you to support your child's developing math skills. Some math and science skills that are important in the toddler and preschool years include

- Demonstrating an interest in numbers (counting and recognizing number symbols)
- Using one-to-one correspondence
- Using standard and nonstandard forms of measurement
- Participating in measuring activities (such as during cooking projects)
- Using positional words (under, beside, behind)
- Demonstrating interest in the more/less concept
- Sorting by at least three attributes (color, shape, size)
- Beginning to notice patterns, copying patterns, and initiating patterns

Of course, school-age children are able to participate in higher-level math activities. Your school-age child should be involved in solving problems like "How many cookies should we bake if each person wants two and we have four people in our family?" Encourage your older child to write down the problem and draw a picture of the solution. One of our jobs as parents is to find out what skills our children are working on in school and to provide opportunities for them to practice those skills. Project work is a wonderful way to provide that practice. Don't forget to document your child's use of these skills. Collecting his work and putting that math problem he worked out into the project scrapbook or a display shows that you value your child's growing ability to use academic skills.

Constructing Play Environments

In addition to small models such as block constructions, children will sometimes make large constructions using large boxes that are transformed into the topic under investigation. Many refrigerator boxes have become trains, planes, cars, fire trucks, and tractors. Remember the old saying, "Forget the toy, and just give them the box!" Often these box constructions will later turn into dramatic play environments as your child begins to play in what he made.

PAINTING

Painting is another way that children show what they are learning, although parents are often reluctant to encourage it. Yes, it is a little messy, but children (and grown-ups too) love to paint, and it is a beautiful way to represent what they are learning. Painting is a natural extension of the drawing process and a way to add color and details to pictures. Some suggestions for keeping the mess to a minimum are

- Paint where water is accessible
- Use an inexpensive plastic tablecloth to cover the floor
- Start with washable tempera paints and use an old shirt as a smock

Make sure you offer your child a variety of sizes of paintbrushes, especially very small ones for detail work. You can also encourage your child to experiment with different ways of painting. Will rollers cover smoothly? Will sponges look like the sky? What will happen if you draw first and then add paint?

Even very young children are capable of painting. It is helpful to ask your child to tell you about her painting rather than asking "What is that?" If you then write down your child's words, she will probably tell you more. It is often in this description and elaboration of the painting that you can see your child's understanding of the topic.

SCULPTING

Part of the study of a topic, especially for young children, is the collection and examination of artifacts (or objects) related to the topic. Children are often fascinated with equipment (such as a tire pump), pieces of the item (such as the insides of a radio), clothing that adults use when working (such as an apron or a hat), and tools (such as hammers). When studying real artifacts or tools that adults use, children will often want new ways of representing the same thing. For example, during the Dentist Project in a classroom, children drew the dentist tools, and, using modeling clay, they sculpted them as well.

Parents can find inexpensive clay at most discount stores like Target or Wal-Mart. If this will be the first time your family has worked with clay, you might want to start with a modeling compound that allows air-drying. It is more pliable, and once it has air-dried, your child can paint the sculptures with tempera paint. Once your child feels comfortable using this material, try using real earthen clay (found

Drew was fascinated by the real dental tools that he explored, and he spent many days sculpting them out of clay.

at most hobby stores). This will provide a completely new experience for the family, and the sculptures can be air-dried or fired in a kiln if you have access to one. Sometimes the local elementary school will help with this, especially if your children attend that school. Some tips for encouraging meaningful clay experiences are

- Provide some type of flat surface for working with the clay, like a cutting board or piece of heavy cardboard
- Position the artifact you are trying to model near the clay work area for reference
- Sculpt along with your child and do some problem solving aloud: "I wonder how I can get this leg to stay on?"

Using clay tools like hammers and wire and water for joining makes the experience more authentic and helps young children experience success.

READING AND WRITING

Phase Two of project work offers many opportunities to engage your child in literacy activities. When children are interested in a topic and want to find out more about it, books are a natural resource for their investigations. When they want to label and describe their constructions and drawings, writing is a natural way for them to represent what they are learning. You can support these early literacy attempts by becoming a partner in your child's investigations and by modeling the reading and writing processes. Chapter 8 will give you more ideas of how you might do this.

Extending Project Work

As children investigate a topic, they will become more and more involved in the topic. The topic may narrow. For example, a project on water may take a turn when your child encounters boats. Suddenly boats are the most interesting aspect of the topic. When this appears to happen, just follow your child's lead. You will probably want to help your child develop new questions that relate to this aspect of the project. This will mean that you will also want to identify more field sites and more experts to interview. There will also be more representations (drawings, play episodes, constructions, models, and paintings) produced.

When this happens, it is project work at its best because it indicates that your child is doing in-depth investigation. He may be developing a true interest. There have been projects that continue going from one aspect of the topic to another for a year or more. More often the child's interest will eventually begin to wane, and you will want to provide an opportunity to develop a sense of completion or closure to the project and to celebrate your child's learning. This is Phase Three, which we discuss in Chapter 6. First, we suggest you read about the Mexican Bakery Project and notice especially the activities of the family in Phase Two of their project.

MEXICAN BAKERY PROJECT

PHASE ONE

The Mexican Bakery Project began when Concepción, age 4, expressed an interest in baking. Luz, her mother, noticed her interest and initiated discussions, recipe readings, and drawing with Concepción and her brother Ervin, who was in second grade. Concepción helped her mother cook when she could. She especially enjoyed baking. The family decided to do a project on cooking, specifically on baking.

PHASE TWO

Luz talked with Concepción about baking and was surprised by how much she knew. Concepción made some drawings about baking with her brother Ervin. Luz made cards of the words about baking that Concepción knew so that she could copy them and learn to read them. She also showed Concepción how to bake a specific food.

Luz thought that a good place to visit would be the *panadería*, the bakery, in their town. This bakery made traditional Mexican breads and cakes. Luz talked to the owners of the bakery, and they suggested that the family come when the ovens were not running so they could go behind the counter to see the cooking area.

Luz, Concepción, and Ervin went on the field-site visit. They learned about the process of baking large numbers of rolls and other items. They were able to see how the dough was mixed, where the dough was put to rise, how the dough was cut, and where it went in the ovens. They took pictures of the bakery and all the equipment, focusing on each piece individually.

On their kitchen table, Ervin and Concepción drew pictures about cooking and baking using materials in their art kit.

Concepción and Ervin visited the bakery when the ovens were off so they could go behind the counters and into the baking area to see the equipment.

Photographs, like this one of the walk-in freezer with the rolling racks for baked goods, enable children to study objects and places when they return home.

When they came home, Martin, Concepción and Ervin's father, was very interested in their visit and what they had seen. They looked at the pictures and as a family decided to create models of the baking equipment using scraps around the house and materials in their art box. It took the children three days to re-create the equipment they had seen. They referred to the photos of the equipment again and again to remember what the pieces looked like, and they talked about how each worked. Luz and Martin were learning the English words for the equipment.

Close-up photographs of equipment are often prized by children because they show construction details not usually included in books and other resources.

The mixer that Concepción and Ervin made shows their understanding of the size of the real mixer and how it mixes the dough by stirring.

The finished freezer made from a cereal box has another box inside that the children used to represent the rolling racks for baked goods. Discarded items spur creativity.

Concepción proudly shows her clay sculptures of bakery items.

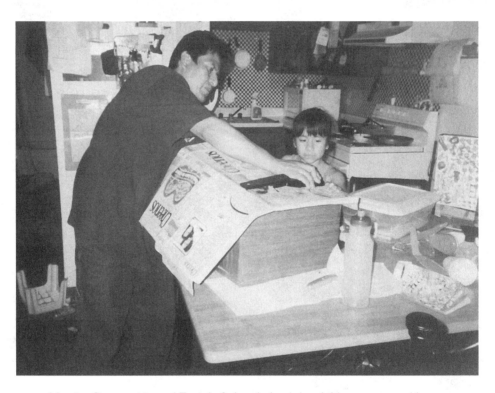

Martin, Concepción and Ervin's father, helped the children cut cereal boxes to make a model of the panadería for play.

The finished bakery with equipment the children made became a favorite toy of Concepción and Ervin.

When the equipment had parts such as gears and levers, they used the insides of discarded clocks and other mechanical items to create the illusion of working motors. They made a freezer with trays for the dough, the oven, the dough cutter, the mixer, and a table. They then made bread, rolls, and other pastries out of the clay in their art box and put the pieces on cardboard trays that went into the freezer and also into the oven.

Martin then helped Concepción and Ervin create a miniature *panadería* out of cereal boxes so that the children could use the constructed equipment to "play bakery." They made the lid so it lifted up like a doll house and cut doors that opened.

Phase Three

The whole family was proud of their creation. The model bakery was taken to school and shared in Concepción's class. Concepción told the other children about each piece of equipment and then played bakery with the other children. Photographs were taken so that everyone could remember the Bakery Project.

SIX

Phase Three: Celebrating the Learning

Eventually there will come a point when a project ends. Your child may have lost interest in a topic, you may have tired of the topic, or you may have exhausted the resources to learn about the topic. You may mistake this waning of interest as failure of the project. However, all projects come to an end. The shifting away of attention to other things in your child's life is natural and to be expected. It also indicates that in many ways your child has satisfied her curiosity and is ready to think about new things.

Sometimes your child will have learned as much as he can at a level he can understand. For example, your 5-year-old child may be interested in planes. You may have visited the airport, read about planes, built model planes, and talked to a person who repairs planes. To go into the topic of planes at a greater depth would require the ability to read books that are more advanced or to study the principles of flight—activities that are beyond your child's abilities. Or you may find that this is a topic that your child will revisit as he matures. Planes and flying may become a lifelong interest of your child. Though a topic may have been of high interest and may have potential for future interest, at some point you will want to wrap up a project. If your child returns to the project later, it will probably have a different focus. For example, a later project topic might be airports.

When you are ready to bring the project to a sense of closure, you will be entering Phase Three. When time is taken to finish a project in a meaningful way, we call that *culminating* the project. Culmination is an important part of project work. There are numerous reasons why closure is needed and numerous ways to allow closure to happen.

The decision to end a project may be made by you or by your child. A child will often signal the end of the project by showing little or no interest in further exploring the topic. If your child goes for more than a week without talking about the topic, then it is probably time to culminate the project. It is important to end the project with some sense of finality. Stopping a project without culmination does not allow for a specific point of closure. Just as a quilter puts all of the squares together to see the finished quilt, a culminating activity can help you and your child see the final, combined fruits of your efforts. You and your child have committed time and energy to the project, and you need time to reflect on and relish all that you have done and learned through the activities. To drop a project suddenly without reflection robs you and your child of the chance to savor a sense of accomplishment and to talk about your child's achievements. This is a wonderful opportunity for your child to get meaningful feedback from others, which will build his self-esteem. It will also enable you and your child to celebrate working together, being a team.

It is important not to wait too long to culminate a project. You do not want your child to become bored with the topic. As the two of you look back on the project, you want your child to remember learning with enthusiasm and enjoyment. If the topic is a chore or has become a painful activity, you and your child will not have a positive disposition toward learning or for future project work. Finally, culmination allows your child to reflect on what went well during the project and what things she may want to do differently in the future. For example, if painting Play Dough was a mess, perhaps your child will be interested in exploring colored modeling clay during the next project. While grade school children may be better able to articulate what went well and what they may try in the future, with some parent coaching young children can make suggestions for future improvements and activities. One of the best things about culminating activities is that they help wrap the project up into what often becomes a child's treasured memories of family time spent together.

Filled with pride, Grandma and Kaylin displayed their final project—a Cinderella pillow.

Documentation

As you have moved through the project, hopefully you have been saving evidence of all of the exciting learning experiences that occurred. In your first projects, collecting the evidence will probably fall along a continuum. On one end of the scale, some parents will keep every scrap of paper from every activity along with taking rolls and rolls of pictures. On the other end of the scale, some parents may throw many things away, thinking that at the end of the project there might be one final special thing they will want to keep. The most beneficial collection would fall somewhere in the middle of the continuum.

Taking some photos, keeping Time 1 and Time 2 drawings, and perhaps taking some notes will allow the story of the project to be saved without becoming overwhelming as the family reflects on the project. Below is a list of some types of evidence of learning you will want to watch for as you work through the project:

- *Webs.* As you and your child talked about what is known about the topic and what you want to explore, writing notes and making webs helps document the growth that occurred during the project. You can also start the web in one color and then use a new color to record additional knowledge your child has gained.

The information learned during the Plant Project was shared through a mural.

- *Lists.* Perhaps when you went on the field-site visit you took a list of questions for your expert or made a list of things you observed at the field site. Even in their rough forms, these lists are reminders of field site information.
- *Language Products.* Things like journals, notes, your child's recollections, and so forth all serve as important documentation of activities and learning. These may include rough, handwritten notes and thoughts and do not need to be polished to be valuable.
- *Drawings.* As your child makes first and second attempts at observation drawings, watch for ones you could collect. Remember the first attempts should be rough and might not represent what your child is trying to draw. Typically, you will see growth in your child as she explores the topic over time.
- *Paintings.* Similar to drawings, painted representations of learning can be saved. Your child might not have a second attempt at the painting, but the use of a different medium is an attractive addition to the documentation.
- *Constructions/Models.* Depending on the size, a model or construction may be savable (think clay dog) or may have to be captured in photographs (think bulldozer made out of a large cardboard box). Typically, models and constructions take a significant amount of time and effort, and you will naturally want to save some evidence of the work.

By collecting these items and organizing them in some fashion, you will create a treasured journal of an activity that was meaningful to you and your child and

Joshua and Caleb shared their mural of slimy animals during an open house for their family, as well as drawings and clay structures they had made.

Gordon and his dad created a papier mâché representation of their dog Maude.

perhaps even your entire family. The Family Project Planning Journal at the end of this book is designed to not only guide the project process but also to serve as a convenient way to document what is happening in the project. Photocopied and placed in a three-ring binder with blank pages and protector pockets, the journal can be an excellent record of the experience. As your child looks through the journal and at photos, he may be inspired to start thinking about his next topic or project activities. When you organize these items and show how they will be preserved, your child realizes that his work is important and valued. This strengthens the child's self-concept and disposition toward learning. More than verbal praise, seeing his work and reflecting on all that has been learned fosters a sense of accomplishment and pride.

Culminating Activities

Beyond the use of the journal and some discussion with your child, a project may also be culminated in a way that invites others to see what you have done and learned. This may not be appropriate for every project, and some projects may lend themselves more to this type of culmination than others. Imagine this scenario:

You and your child have been working on a project about birds. Birds have fascinated your child, and you have spent hours learning about birds in your area. Together you have learned to identify birds visually and have taken trips to the local nature center and forest preserve to gain more knowledge. During your work, your child has created drawings, the two of you have taken many photos, and your child has even made models of birds using clay. You and your child have made lists of birds you have studied and webs of the questions you have explored. You have finally decided to wrap up the project.

What could you do to culminate the learning and share what you have learned? Fortunately, culminating the project is as open ended as the project itself, and you and your child are limited only by your creativity and the amount of effort you want to put into the event! The following are just a few ideas of how the Bird Project could be culminated:

- *Create a display.* Using your dining room table for a week or two, the pictures, models, lists, and webs could be displayed for family and friends. With more effort, you and your child could mount it on foam core boards for a more permanent display. Using magnets, the refrigerator can become a display board.
- *Make a scrapbook.* The documentation could be neatly placed in a scrapbook or some type of album. Again, your family, relatives, and friends could have access to the album to share in your celebration of learning. This would tell the story of the project—what your child did, what was learned, where you went, and so forth.
- *Make a book.* Some projects lend themselves well to making a picture or story book. For example, a culminating activity for the Bird Project might be making a bird book. Your child could put paintings or drawings of the different birds you learned about in a book. Young children could dictate words about birds. School-age children could write their own information.
- *Make a video.* Depending on your technical knowledge and your child's desire to share on camera, you may want to video your child talking about all of the items from the project. Like a museum tour, she can share information about birds, describe the individual artifacts, and answer questions from the off-screen audience (probably you).
- *Make a CD.* If your family has access to a computer and digital camera, any of the project work can be collected using a presentation program such as KidPix or even PowerPoint. School-age children will find this especially meaningful. The presentation can be saved on a CD and also emailed to relatives.
- *Do a presentation for neighbors or relatives.* Much like the video, your child can serve as the neighborhood bird expert, sharing all of her new knowledge about birds. This presentation need not be long or technical, but it gives your little expert a time to shine as she fields questions and describes activities and accomplishments.
- *Share in school.* If your child is in school, he may want to take some of his work to school. Teachers can encourage your child's interest in his project.

While inviting your neighbors or grandparents into your home for a presentation might seem a little unusual, these activities are no different from inviting your neighbor to watch a video of your daughter's dance recital or asking grandpa and grandma to watch your child play in a baseball game. These opportunities not only allow your child's work to be shared, they also help educate others about the importance of making learning meaningful for your child. They also enable children to relate to other adults in meaningful ways and to have meaningful conversations with them.

Don't forget to share some of the products of this phase with those who gave of their time to help your child with his project. A photo of your child and his expert or a photocopy of a picture that your child has painted or drawn can be given as a thank you. As teachers, we have often seen how being an expert for a project has changed adults' minds about what children can understand and do. Often experts will come to see displays, visit with children, and tell others about project work. Consider yourself an educator and visionary as you teach others

To share their learning with family, the Slime Project was displayed throughout the house as family listened to the children describe their project work and saw their experiments and creations.

about the importance of spending quality time with children. Perhaps they will pass on to others how you and your child created shared experiences and treasured family memories and encourage others to invest in their child and family.

Reflecting on the Project

As you end your project, it is helpful for you the colearner to take time to reflect on the project experience for you and your child. In Chapter 1, we suggested that there were benefits of project work for both you and your child. You can see if you have realized these benefits by thinking about the following questions.

QUESTIONS ABOUT YOUR CHILD

1. Did this project contribute to your child's intellectual development? Did he think about the topic in meaningful ways? Did he come up with questions? Were there problems that your child solved?
2. Could your child see the value of reading, writing, and using math skills? Were these skills practiced? Were there any academic skills such as measuring or using books for research that your child learned or practiced in this project?
3. Did your child show initiative in the project work? Were you able to see him thinking, using his mind? Did your child show curiosity? Did you see him con-

sciously try to learn, analyze, theorize, hypothesize, or make predictions?

4. Did your child recognize her own contribution? Did she grow in self-confidence or self-esteem through this project?

5. Did your child grow in her sense of connection to the world and what is going on in that world? Did she learn more about her family, neighborhood, or city and the people in it?

6. Did your child get to know you better? Did he see you as a support and a teammate?

7. Did your child enjoy the project? Was it worth her time to participate in the project work?

QUESTIONS ABOUT YOU

1. Did the project provide a reason or means for you to set aside time for meaningful interaction with your child? Did you make it happen?

2. Were you able to model and strengthen dispositions that you want your child to have, such as "to want to read," "to be curious," "to be persistent"? Were you able to pass on any of your own interests or values to your child through the project work?

3. Were you able to let your child lead—to follow your child's interest and curiosity and not take over the project?

4. Did you learn anything new during this project? Did you find yourself intellectually stimulated and more interested in the topic as you saw it through your child's eyes? Were you able to focus on the project experience with your child and break from thinking about day-to-day demands?

5. Did you grow in your sense of connection to the world and what is going on in that world? Did you learn anything new about your family, neighborhood, or city and the people in it?

6. Did you see your child grow and develop? Did you see your child's strengths and interests? Do you have a better idea of who your child is as a person? Do you feel closer to your child?

Final Questions

The following questions are for all those who participated in the project: Was this a good, meaningful, and enjoyable shared learning experience? Beyond the academic skills, dispositions, and intellectual skills developed in the project, did this project provide a fun learning experience that brought you closer to each other and built a shared memory? If it did, then perhaps in today's busy world that, in and of itself, is enough.

As you read the story of the Horse Project, which follows this chapter, notice how fun was mixed with learning for Ashley and Ryan.

H O R S E
P R O J E C T

P H A S E   O N E

The entire Hoefft family—4-and-a-half-year-old Ashley, 2-year-old Ryan, and their mom and dad—participated in this project. Ashley was born with Cerebral Palsy and has many motor challenges. After participating in a project in her preschool, Ashley began talking with her mom and Ryan about topic possibilities for a project at home.

After they examined some photographs taken on Ashley's preschool trip to a local farm, they decided they wanted to know more about horses. They made a preliminary web, with Mom doing the writing and Ashley and Ryan supplying the ideas. The web listed the parts of the horse (ears, legs, head), and the fact that horses can be ridden. (The web can be seen in Chapter 4.) The family looked for books about horses and used those books for references as the children drew some preliminary sketches. Ashley and Ryan performed a puppet show for their parents about horses. They also spent many sessions at the kitchen table "writing notes" about horses.

Ashley was highly motivated to write words during the Horse Project. Here she is writing "a note about horses."

"note about horses"

Ashley

Ashley's note.

One unplanned event that happened in Phase One was that while in the car running errands, the family decided to drive around and see if they could find any horses. They came upon a horse in a field and stopped to observe. Ashley's mom provided the following conversation from this family event:

ASHLEY: Let's go see horses!
RYAN: I want ride pony, too!
MOM: We aren't riding today, just looking at what they do and taking pictures.
RYAN: Ride on back.
MOM: Where do we ride on horses, on what part of their bodies?
ASHLEY: Their backs.

There was lots of excitement about this trip. We drove around the country looking for horses.

ASHLEY: Look for fences.
RYAN: Look for horsey.

We found a horse on Hickory Grove Road and pulled over to observe.

MOM: Look at what the horse is doing.
ASHLEY: It's standing. Uh-oh, it is walking.
RYAN: A horsey.
ASHLEY AND RYAN: Hi, horsey!
ASHLEY: It's coming to us!! She's peeing.
MOM: Where does the horse live?
ASHLEY: A farm, that barn.
RYAN: A barn.
ASHLEY: Let's see if we can find another horse. The barn is red.
MOM: Let's look at the horse close-up. Don't touch. Look at her toes.
ASHLEY: It's a mommy horse!
RYAN: It's a daddy horse!
MOM: Look at its face. What is that on its face? *(The horse had on a halter.)*
ASHLEY: I don't know.
RYAN: Cold!

We returned home, and Ashley got out the pens and notebooks for her and Ryan to write in.

MOM: What are you doing?
ASHLEY: Just writing a note about horses. Horses that you see.
RYAN: Horses too mommy.
ASHLEY: A few more words.
RYAN: Make note-note.

P H A S E   T W O

The children were involved in lots of dramatic play using stick horses. They would pretend to feed the horses, brush them, and, of course, ride them. Some of their initial questions included

> What are baby horses called?
> (What are) Mommy and Daddy horses (called)?
> Where do horses sleep?
> What do they eat?
> How come we got to take care of horses?
> Do they poop standing up or sitting down?

Ashley's interest in writing grew, and she expressed an interest in labeling the parts of a horse. Using a plastic model, Ashley drew the horse and then labeled the parts she knew. As Ryan watched his big sister, he, too, wanted paper to "write" and did his writing alongside Ashley.

The family planned a field experience to a local horse stable, and they organized clipboards and cameras for the trip. At the stables, Ashley sketched horses and was very interested in exploring all the different foods they ate.

At the end of the morning, Ashley got to ride one of the horses!

Ashley used sticky notes to make labels to show the parts of her toy horse. Her mother made labels for her to use as a guide.

Ashley sketched the horses at the horse barn using the clipboard and materials that her mother packed for them.

"Chart of people who rode horses."

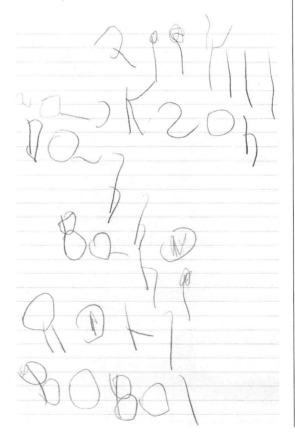

Ashley wrote this chart of people who rode horses. As a 4-year-old, Ashley's letterlike shapes with some correctly formed letters are appropriate for her age level.

When the family returned home, they made a book together that included all the different horse foods that they had investigated at the stables. Mom and Ashley also made a chart that organized which horses were exercised the day they visited and a chart of people who rode the horses.

Ashley wanted to make a list of all the horses' names. There were many writing opportunities for Ashley to develop her fine motor skills, and she was highly motivated to record information by writing words.

P H A S E   T H R E E

The Hoefft family celebrated the culmination of the horse project by inviting the grandparents over so Ashley and Ryan could share what they had learned about horses. They read their book about horse food, displayed their horse drawings, and looked at all the photographs from their stable visit. They ended the evening by viewing *Spirit*, an animated movie about horses.

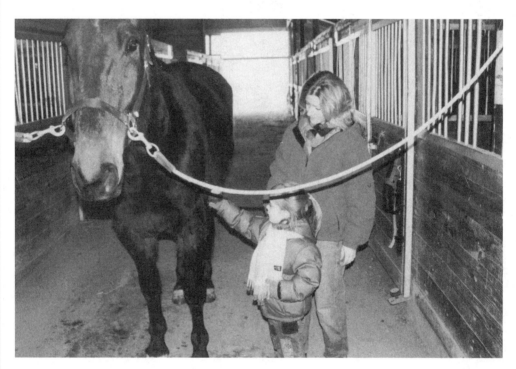

At the end of the project, the family invited grandparents to visit, and they shared favorite photos from the horse barn visit, like this one of Ashley and her mother with the horse.

part III

Expanding Your Knowledge

SEVEN

Understanding Your Child's Development

As parents, we have found our training in child development to be extremely helpful to our parenting. As we studied children in preparation to become teachers, we learned about their typical development at different ages and how we might support that development.

How Can I Support My Child's Growth in Skills?

Most children grow and develop along a trajectory of normal development. For example, children will learn to sit up, then to crawl, and then to walk. When a child does these things is determined by several factors: biological factors (the growth in the child's physical abilities to do certain tasks), cultural expectations, and experiences.

Overall most children grow in ways similar to other children and achieve important milestones at approximately the same time. There are certain accomplishments that we look for at certain age levels. These are often called "widely held expectations." Teachers use them as a guide for interacting with children and for providing learning experiences. Teachers also share these widely held expectations at parent-teacher conferences so that parents and teachers can work together to help a child either continue or accelerate growth in skills.

As a parent, you can be more helpful to your child if you know about developmental milestones of children and carefully observe your child. This will enable you to identify what your child can and cannot do and what she is ready to learn.

Educators often use the term *developmentally appropriate* to describe activities and experiences that are appropriate at certain age levels. For example, we would not expect 3-year-olds to listen to a museum lecture about geology, even though rocks might be of great interest to a specific 3-year-old child. Lectures are developmentally inappropriate for 3-year-olds because, typically, they have difficulty understanding lectures. However, this child could study rocks through hands-on exploration, especially if a museum staff member stood nearby to answer questions conversationally.

By knowing about the typical development of children, you can make experiences more developmentally appropriate for your child. For example, very young children typically attend to books that have photos or pictures and a small amount of text. Knowing this, you could adapt a book about rocks written for middle school children or adults with a lot of text and good photos. You could make it developmentally appropriate and interesting for your preschooler by "reading" the book in a way a younger child can understand (explaining pictures and illustrations and summarizing the text).

Your child's development, however, may be different than that of most children his age. There are a number of reasons why a child's development might not be typical. Children's development can be off the trajectory because of delays. For example, a child who does not hear language clearly because of a hearing problem may speak at a much later age. Or a child may develop motor skills at a later age because most of the children in your family just happen to be slower at developing skills in this area.

A child may also be beyond expectations of the trajectory because of extensive experiences in an area of development. For example, he may begin to read early if there are many books in the home, he is read to extensively, and an adult explains the reading process.

Your child may develop faster in some areas and slower in others. One characteristic of young children is that they do not tend to grow evenly but will often grow in spurts in different areas. For example, a child who is learning to walk may seem slow in learning how to talk because she is putting much concentration and energy into the walking process. A child could be advanced in verbal skills but have difficulty pedaling a tricycle. We also know that if a child is ill or suffers a trauma, the body will naturally attempt to accelerate development until the child is back on the normal trajectory.

Another way to think of *developmentally appropriate* is to think of the appropriateness of experiences for your specific child. You know your child, usually better than teachers do, because you see her in many different situations and at different times in the day. An advantage to doing project work at home is that you can observe your child and match experiences to her developmental level. This is especially true when a child grows up in an environment rich in literacy or representation experiences.

What Does Brain Research Tell Us?

As a parent, you may be interested in research on the brain and what it tells us about your child's development. We have become accustomed to such innovations as CAT scans and DNA analysis and have seen how these have revolutionized many areas of our lives. Many of these same technologies are revolutionizing our understanding of the brain and the development of intelligence. You may wonder how this research affects your role as a parent.

We know so much more now about giftedness, learning problems (such as attention deficit disorder), and how children learn to read. You have more impact

Seth, growing up in a literacy-rich environment and with an older brother who loves to write and draw, is starting to do observational sketching at two, and attempting to label drawings earlier than one would expect.

than you may have realized on your child's intelligence, especially in the early years, and you can indeed make your child "smarter" by the experiences you provide.

Technology has changed our understanding of the brain, and the images of it you have may be outdated. You may have an image of the brain as a computer that records and stores experiences in the form of memory—similar to a hard drive. Another image of the brain is that of a video camera or tape recorder that records via images and sound bites. From our studies of brain research we have abandoned those images and think of the brain more as a living, growing thing that is improved by rest, good nutrition, care, and exercise. Unlike a computer, there is no limit to the amount of information that can be stored. The brain simply creates more connections as new information is learned, which then enables it to be open to more learning. Also, like any living thing it is affected by the environment, toxins, and injury.

The brain takes care of itself in many ways—growing, pruning, and shaping itself to match the environment and the challenges it faces. If that environment is interesting and thought provoking, the brain becomes complex and efficient. However, unlike a video camera or tape recorder, which captures everything, the brain most efficiently captures and stores information when it is meaningful and integrates with what is already known. When your child hears something for the first time, he is unlikely to remember it unless it makes sense and connects with something else he knows. As a leaf grows from the branch rather than separate from it, your child's new knowledge and skills build on previous knowledge and skills. Your role as a parent is to help your child make these connections. When a parent helps a child focus on the similarities and differences between his beagle and the poodle down the street, or points out that the puddle the child splashed in yesterday is ice today, that parent is helping his child make connections.

You may have some difficulty weighing the hype that has come with the discovery of more and more information about how the brain develops. Some of the concepts from brain research that have valid applications to child rearing are

- The early years are important for brain development but are not the only important years
- Children have enormous potential for development—how smart they become is not determined at birth
- Interaction with adults and other children in meaningful ways is probably still the best stimulation we can provide to children
- Children learn to think by thinking, and the more they think, the smarter they become

Experiences that support brain development need not be high technology or bought in a package. Developing a smarter child is a matter of spending time together, paying attention to your child's thinking, interacting with her in meaningful experiences, and providing lots of language and love. The more you challenge your child to think, the better thinker your child will become.

One last note on brain research. "Use it or lose it!" is a valid directive for children of all ages and for adults, too. When parents or grandparents become immersed in learning in project work, the child's brain is not the only one stimulated.

What Dispositions Should I Encourage?

To get your child to do all this good thinking, she needs to see herself as a successful learner. In Chapter 1, we introduced dispositions, which Dr. Lilian Katz explains as "habits of mind." Many dispositions are inborn, such as curiosity, but can be strengthened or weakened by experiences. We think there are many opportunities in project work to strengthen three types of dispositions.

DISPOSITIONS TO USE YOUR MIND

These dispositions are sometimes called "intellectual dispositions." They refer to the willingness and sense of fulfillment that occurs when your child thinks at a high level. Dispositions to use your mind include

- Being curious and deeply engaged
- Trying to make the best sense of experiences
- Analyzing and closely examining reality and its complexities
- Developing theories
- Hypothesizing what may happen or what might have happened
- Being willing to make predictions

These intellectual dispositions enable children to do well in school and later in jobs because they are motivated to think.

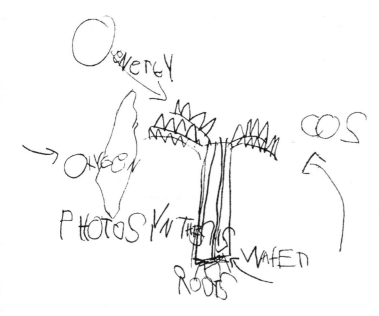

Audrey copied this diagram about photosynthesis at the age of 4 during a family project on plants. Although we can't be sure how much Audrey truly understands, we do know she has a strong disposition to figure things out and to use books to help her find the answers to questions.

DISPOSITIONS TO WORK HARD

These habits of mind refer to how well children are motivated to work or to do good work. They include dispositions to

- Learn something new even if it takes effort
- Use representation skills such as drawing even if it is difficult
- Use literacy skills such as reading, writing, and researching in books even though these skills may be new
- Use numbers and number thinking to solve problems rather than just guessing or giving up
- Evaluate their work and see how they can improve
- Listen attentively to suggestions from others
- Be persistent in learning something or solving a problem

These work dispositions also enable children to be successful at school tasks and later in a career.

DISPOSITIONS TO WORK WITH OTHERS

Dr. Katz talks about children learning how to work with others, how to appreciate contributions of others, and how to nurture others through project work in classrooms. Even though project work in families is often a project of a single child, there are ways that these dispositions can be strengthened in family projects as well. These dispositions include

- Listening to the ideas of others
- Appreciating the contributions that others make to our well-being
- Appreciating diversity in cultures
- Compromising
- Supporting those who are having difficulty learning
- Working together as a team
- Sharing credit with others for work well done

There are opportunities for all of these dispositions to work with others to be strengthened when there are siblings who become involved in project work. Even if your child works on a project alone, he can develop dispositions of appreciation of the work of others and their culture. Your child can recognize the importance of teamwork when he observes adults working together or listens to adults describe how they accomplish a task.

How Do I Strengthen Dispositions?

Parental modeling of these positive dispositions is a very effective way to strengthen your child's dispositions. When your child sees that you have questions and are using your mind, she will want to do the same. When your child sees you getting excited about something you have learned and did not know before, then he will become excited also. If you get a charge out of seeing the back area of the local grocery store right along with your child, then you are modeling interest in life and what is happening in her world.

One of the best ways to strengthen intellectual dispositions is to engage your child in meaningful conversation. Look closely at objects and ask your child to look with you. You can then tell each other what you see. For example, during a project on elephants, you might ask your child to guess what he thinks elephants might eat. Or, on a trip to the zoo you could model how you develop your own theories, such as, "I think maybe elephants eat hay because there appears to be a lot of hay in that box." You can ask you child to observe and develop his own theory, such as, "Looking at the elephant yard, what do you think elephants eat?"

You can also help your child test out his ideas by finding more information. For example, you might find a sign describing the elephant, and on the sign it might say what elephants eat. By taking time to think, come up with your own ideas, and then find out the answer, you are helping your child develop strategies for thinking.

You can have your child predict things, like how many tires there are on a fire truck. With a school-age child, you might ask her to predict quantities such as how many shopping carts a store might have, or how the color is applied to cars during car repair. The idea is to help your child develop the dispositions to wonder, to predict, and to come up with theories by modeling or by challenging your child in appropriate ways. This can become a fun part of project work if you keep the predictions and thinking challenges appropriate to the age level of the child.

Dispositions can be strengthened when your child has an opportunity to experience them and recognize the positive feelings they generate. For example, when your child finds the answer to a project question in a book, she has a sense of satisfaction. This will make it more likely that she will look in a book for answers in the future. She will also think that books are valuable and that reading is a valuable skill for her to learn. Similarly, when a child has difficulty accomplishing a task and has to try several times but finally does accomplish it, he learns that persistence pays off and that a person can feel very good when he solves a difficult problem.

It is important that your child have these experiences in an active way. That is, your child needs to think about looking for the answer in the book, finding the book, and then finding the answer. Your child needs to figure out the answer to the problem. That means that in order to strengthen many of the dispositions you would like to come out of project work, you need to let your child take the lead as much as possible and not step in too soon.

Another way to strengthen these important dispositions is to give voice to them during project work. You can observe how your child worked hard to find a solution to a representation problem and was then successful. One way to do this is for you to take photos and talk about first attempts as well as the following successful attempts. Then you can look at the pictures and talk with your child about how he was persistent and how he was able to figure out what to do in the end. You can talk about how that happens to adults also and how important it is to keep trying.

You can also give voice to feelings of accomplishment and fulfillment that you feel when new information is learned. For example, you might say, "It was really fun to see that elephant and find out what the zoo keeper fed him. I had no idea that elephants ate that much! That was amazing!" You can also reflect your child's feelings, "That mural of the truck was very big and took a lot of time. You must feel proud that you stuck with that and got it done."

Giving voice to your feelings and helping your child use words to describe feelings is one way to be sure that she becomes more aware of her accomplishments. As your child thinks, "Yes, I did work hard," or "Yes, I did solve that problem," she becomes conscious of accomplishments and growing skills and knowledge. This focus on a child's accomplishments leads to the development of positive self-esteem and self-confidence.

What Is the Difference between Encouragement and Praise?

Talking about your child's accomplishments need not lead to excessive praise. Too much praise will make your child self-centered and decrease the joy that he feels in accomplishing goals for his own self-satisfaction. As teachers, we see a difference between encouragement and praise. When praising a child, adults often make positive comments about the child's work, such as "Great job!" or "Pretty picture," or even "I really like that!" The problem with these general statements of praise is that they focus the child on gaining the approval of others rather than on strengthening other dispositions. Praise is very global, a statement of overall approval. Although your child will often react positively to praise like this, she tends to get accustomed to it, and it is easy for you to slip into pretending to look at or evaluate what your child has done and responding automatically. You child can recognize "inattentive" attention (pretending you are paying attention when you really aren't). This kind of praise also often becomes dishonest, and your child can recognize that, too.

Encouragement, however, goes beyond praise to providing specific comments and constructive help. The difference between encouragement and praise can be seen in this example about baseball. Imagine yourself as the player. After you strike out, the coach could offer you two comments. The first is "That's okay. You are really a fantastic ballplayer. This was just bad luck." The second is "You tried hard. Next time, choke up on the bat, and step into the pitch." Which comment is more helpful to a player wanting to improve? Even though the first comment is very positive, it might not have been honest. You, as the ballplayer, probably recognized that it wasn't honest. The second comment is not completely positive; however, it recognizes effort and provides information for future improvement. When you come up to bat next time, which comment might help you achieve a more positive result? As you work with your child, you will have similar situations.

As part of encouraging children, we try not to be globally positive. Instead of telling your child his drawing is "good" or "pretty," you might say something similar to the following:

"It is cool the way you included all the levers in your drawing of the tractor."
"Look at that. I can see how you were thinking of how the word *tractor* starts with a T sound when you wrote this!"
"How could you change this drawing of our dog's ear to make it more like Sparky's?"

Children appreciate evaluation when it is given in a caring, meaningful way. When you provide specific feedback—even when it is constructive criticism—it shows your child that you feel her work is important and you want to take time to assess what she is doing.

At times, your child might become very frustrated with what he is doing during project work. Perhaps the clay just will not cooperate, or the glue is just not sticking. You will come to these crossroads and will need to make a decision about how to guide your child. There is a fine line between pushing your child to try just a little harder and pushing your child into frustration. Reading your child's patience level will be an important skill in knowing when to say, "Let's try something else," or even, "Let's take a break from this today." Project work is meant to be a positive learning experience, not a punishment that ends with tears of frustration and disappointment.

Using your verbal skills to talk your child through problem-solving strategies may be helpful. Instead of allowing negative emotions to take over, you might help your child assess the situation by using some of these phrases:

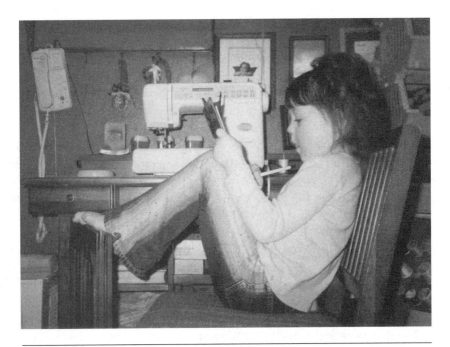

When a child has a strong interest in a topic, like Kaylin does in sewing, she will benefit from encouragement and an honest and open discussion about her work.

"Can you tell me what the problem is?"
"Are there some other ideas that you could try?"
"Maybe you could think about . . . ."

These comments encourage the child to come up with a solution or at least a next step.

Sometimes your child might be facing a representation problem, or he has come to a point where he has tried all of his ideas and doesn't know what else he could possibly do. Then it might be appropriate to say

"This will not work because. . . . Why don't you try. . . ."
"I wonder if ____ might have some ideas you could try."

It is important that your child learn that just because a task is challenging does not mean that he needs to scrap the whole project or give up on his skills. Encouragement can help your child develop the dispositions to try to solve problems, to listen to others, and to be persistent.

Encouragement also strengthens your child's dispositions to improve the quality of her work. During the process of project work, there is a time when a child's work needs to be accepted and a time when a child needs to be asked to try a little harder. Again, you have to know your child and be aware of her skills and talents. You want to foster a positive attitude and not kill enthusiasm for the project, but you also want to have high expectations for your child. As your child works, there may be times when you say, "I think you should try that part again," or "Is that your best work?" Perhaps your child will say, "No, I don't want to try again," or "Yes, that is my best work." Since this is project work and you are doing it for fun, we would not recommend pushing a child on this issue. Even if she does not make any changes, you are still modeling the disposition to self-evaluate and improve work. As the child matures or becomes more vested in a project, she is often willing to try again or to tweak details in her work. Later, as an older student, she will become more conscientious as a learner about putting forth her best effort and feeling satisfied with her effort as a learner.

In the story of the Bus Project that follows this chapter, you will see how Mary Ann Gottlieb supported the developing dispositions of her 2-year-old grandson, Atticus. She was very sensitive to which activities were appropriate for his level of development. Her knowledge about the typical development of toddlers and the unique characteristics of Atticus enabled her to support his learning and to encourage the development of intellectual dispositions. In Chapter 8 you will learn more specific suggestions for guiding your child's skill development through the process of coaching.

BUS PROJECT

Mary Ann Gottlieb

Atticus, our 2-year-old grandson, stays with us while his parents work. Twice a week Atticus and I travel 36 miles round trip so that he can attend Northminster Learning Center's Curiosity Corner, a preschool program for toddlers 15–23 months. Since we are traveling during the morning rush hour, we see many school buses, both large and small, on our commute. Last fall, we began looking for buses and liked to speculate as to whether or not those buses were going to the school where Atticus's Mama and Dad teach.

PHASE ONE

After attending the first night of the Parents' Project Group seminar, I made a list of topics in which Atticus seemed interested. He certainly talked a lot about buses. "Can I drive it?" he would say over and over. We had, on two separate occasions, met the Peoria Charter Bus arriving from Chicago, and each time we discussed the eminent arrival, Atticus would ask, "Can I touch it?" When we took my sister to catch the bus back to her home, Atticus was very interested in the luggage compartment and watched intensely as the driver loaded the suitcases. We walked around the bus and looked at it closely several times as we waited for its departure. The bus driver allowed us

Atticus and Grandpa look at the door of a school bus in the parking lot of Limestone Community High School.

to get on the bus, and we sat in the seat across from Aunt Laurie Ann. Based on his interest in these experiences, I thought that Atticus would be interested in learning more about buses.

However, Atticus also loved the car. "I drive it," he said time after time as we approached the car. If allowed to get into the car, Atticus would go directly to the steering wheel and really fussed when placed in his car seat. He liked to play with the Matchbox cars that belonged to his uncle. His favorite books where those about cars, trucks, and buses. Grandpa had given him a set of keys, which he carried around, saying, "I drive it," as he searched for places in the house to insert a key. I knew that the car would be a project of intense interest should we pursue it.

And then there was the exercise equipment in the basement. Atticus loved watching Grandpa work out. Grandpa would slow down the treadmill, and Atticus would walk on it while it was barely moving. Every time he went downstairs, Atticus wanted to ride the Exercycle. He wanted to sit on the weight bench and pull the bar down. He wanted to do whatever Grandpa did. Once we were downstairs, Atticus would go directly into the weight room—even when the light was off!

In the meantime, I thought about Stacy Berg's talk regarding a specific location for project work. We do not have a family room or a finished basement. There is no separate room large enough to accommodate a project in process. I finally decided to buy a plastic tub and store the art materials in it. I also bought a larger tub in which to keep materials for constructions and started to add materials to it—pieces of Styrofoam, paper plates, cardboard strips, and so forth.

When I was thinking about the possible topics, I asked my husband to be on the lookout for a large box. I thought we might use it should we choose to make a construction. Grandpa brought home a large box approximately the size of a water heater, and we put it in the living room. Atticus explored the box but was hesitant to crawl inside. It sat in the living room for several days while we began to "mess around" with the topic of buses. We found all the bus books we owned and read them over and over. We sang "The Horn on the Bus" song until Atticus, in his own way, would try to sing it by himself. We looked for buses everywhere we went. We gathered all of his toy vehicles and sorted them by category: buses, trucks, and cars. Aunt Laurie Ann sent us different Matchbox buses.

One Saturday while Atticus was staying with us, we took him to Limestone High School to visit his parents. As we entered the school parking lot, we saw many big buses, some smaller buses, buses from other schools, and one very small bus. We walked around the parking lot, looking at the buses. We identified the parts that Atticus knew: lights, doors, windows, windshield wipers, and tires.

Fortunately, I had brought the camera, so I took as many pictures as possible. Atticus was so excited. I knew we had found the right project.

While Atticus was sleeping, I used my computer to print the pictures I had taken of the buses at Limestone High School and made a bus book for him. I didn't bind it because I wanted him to be able to use the individual pages for reference. We talked about the pictures when he woke up, and when his parents arrived, Atticus excitedly told them about our impromptu parking lot field-site visit.

I still had some concerns about a project on buses. Judy Helm had talked with me once about the importance of artifacts in project work. I tried to make a list of "things" from a bus that we could gather to display at home. I knew that we could get a bus tire but couldn't think of anything else. Judy suggested that I gather as many toy buses as possible and go from there. I started haunting the toy stores, looking for different buses. Eventually, we gathered a school bus, a double-decker bus, an airport shuttle bus, a wooden bus, and a Playskool bus with little wooden "people."

mirror

Mary Ann printed some pictures with vocabulary words under them to help Atticus associate the printed word with a picture of a familiar part of the bus. These photos were assembled into a simple reference book about buses.

Atticus is trying to send this bus down the yardstick ramp after watching Mary Ann place a bus on the yardstick. He was successful after several attempts with different sized buses.

I knew that we could visit a nearby school bus company. I also knew that we could go to Peoria Charter Bus Company, which was located in a nearby city. I decided we could meet the Peoria Charter Bus even if no one was coming to visit. There was also a historical trolley bus that operates in warm weather, which would make an interesting follow-up trip next summer.

I decided that a bus project would be appropriate because Atticus already knew some facts about buses; he continues to see buses every day; and by actually observing real buses, he would be doing his own research. The project was a go.

When Atticus came to our house the next Monday, I pulled the big box into the middle of the floor and asked him if he wanted to make a bus. I knew that he would be unable to create this bus by himself, so I thought that I would ask him what to put on the bus and then I would be the "hands" to create his ideas. We looked at his buses and the bus pictures, and he began to tell me what to do. I got a large knife to cut the cardboard with, and he immediately hopped up into a chair to watch. The following is some of the conversation that accompanied our work:

ATTICUS: Windows.
GRANDMA: How many windows?
ATTICUS: Three.
GRANDMA: Do you want wheels on your bus? How many wheels?
ATTICUS: One, two, three. Make door. Cut door. Close door.

Then Atticus got up and gathered all the "little people" from the Playskool bus. He put them inside the bus saying, "People sit down." And then began singing, "People on bus go up and down."

ATTICUS: Make window. Turn it over.
GRANDMA (turning the box over to the other side): "Do you want windows on this side?"
ATTICUS: One, two, three.
GRANDMA: Shall we make a window for the driver?
ATTICUS: Yea. Sure. OK.

He stood at the front of the box and touched the cardboard. I made the driver's window there. Atticus went into the bus and tried to close the door. Each time, it would pop back open. This happened several times. Finally I said, "What's the matter? Won't the door close?"

ATTICUS: No. Make wheels.
          Grandma, I get out.
          My close door. (He stepped back and looked at the bus.)
          Big school bus, big bus.
          School bus.

Atticus climbed into the chair as Mary Ann began to cut out the window of the bus. He was reluctant to get near the large knife that Mary Ann was using to cut the cardboard.

Grandma, make wheels.
Make wheels.
(yelling) Make wheels!

GRANDMA: How shall we make the wheels?

ATTICUS *(climbing out and pushing the bus)*: Bus driver going.
Time get out, bus driver.
Get out.

GRANDMA: Do we need a window on the back of the bus?

ATTICUS: Yea.

GRANDMA: Get your bus and see. *(Atticus found his biggest bus and looked at it.)*

ATTICUS: Yea, yea.
My bus driver.

GRANDMA: OK. Shall I cut a window on the back?

ATTICUS: Yea. OK. *(He climbed up in the chair again.)*
No, Grandma, No.

GRANDMA: Do you want to show me where to put the window in the back?
Where is the back of the bus?

ATTICUS: Right there. *(He pointed to the back of the bus.)*

GRANDMA: Shall I make a big window or a little window?

ATTICUS: Big, big window, Grandma. Big window.

GRANDMA: Shall I draw it first?

ATTICUS: Yea.

GRANDMA: Like this? *(I drew a big window.)*

ATTICUS: Yea. *(I began to cut the window.)*
Big box. Big box.
My bus. I watching. I watching.
Wheels? Wheels?

GRANDMA: Right. Wheels. How many wheels? *(no response)* What kind of wheels? *(I started singing the song, "The Horn on the Bus Goes Beep, Beep, Beep.")* Do we have a horn?

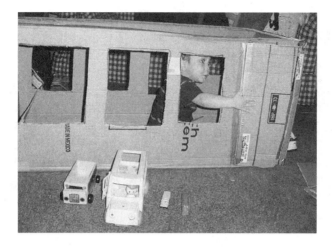

Atticus lined up all his toy buses next to the construction.

We made a list of what we still needed: steering wheel, wheels, windshield wipers, horn, and lights.

Atticus played in the bus on and off for the rest of the day. The door would not stay closed and this seemed to concern him. Atticus pushed the door, hit it, and tried to close it from the inside. Finally, he discovered that if he pushed in the door at the top, it would hold. He was satisfied with this method of closing the door.

The next day I put out some small plastic cups along with Scotch tape, masking tape, and duct tape. Atticus repeatedly said, "Make lights, Grandma, make lights." Grandpa looped the duct tape into pieces and attached the cups as lights to the bus. Atticus took them off and tried to attach them again. When they wouldn't stay on, he turned his attention to something else.

One day while in the kitchen playing with a bowl, a whisk, and a ladle, Atticus took the ladle into the other room and standing in front of the bus, said, "Wiper, Grandma. Wiper. Wiper." I gave him some strips of masking tape, and he managed to attach the ladle to the front window.

One morning we made plans to visit the Peoria Charter Bus Company. When we arrived, we walked from the parking lot to the waiting lounge where the front of a bus protrudes from the building. We walked around the protrusion, looking at and touching the lights, windshield wipers, windows, and door. Atticus seemed very interested in feeling everything, especially the lights.

We then proceeded toward two buses parked outside the storage bays. Atticus became cautious and then frightened. He hid behind me, saying "Too big, Grandma, too big." I stopped and picked him up, and we stood there, near the buses, talking about how big they were.

"Go home, Grandma, go home." Atticus said as he clung to me. So we returned to the car with Atticus frequently looking back at the buses and repeating, "Go home, Grandma, go home."

While playing in the kitchen, Atticus took the soup ladle into the living room and called, "Wiper, Grandma. Wiper! Wiper!" He used masking tape to attach the ladle to the front window of the bus.

I put Atticus back into his car seat and got into the car myself, talking all the time about the buses. I tried to reassure him that buses were big—very big. I took some pictures through the front window of the car, and then we left, with Atticus repeating yet again, "Go home, Grandma, go home."

As I reflect back on this experience, I realize that I should have been talking about the size of the buses all along. I hadn't done that since the last time we had been near the Peoria charter buses when we had picked up or dropped off visiting family members. I was totally surprised that Atticus was frightened. We do not plan to return to Peoria Charter Bus Company's bus barn until summer, when he is a little older, although we will continue to go there to meet our relatives.

On another day, I got out a yardstick and propped it up against the couch. Then I placed a small toy bus at the top of the stick and let it roll down. Atticus immediately came over and tried to do the same thing with a larger bus, but it was too large to balance on the yardstick. Another bus fell off instead of rolling down. Then he picked up a Matchbox bus and down it rolled. He was not able to explain what was happening, but he smiled as he watched the Matchbox bus roll down the yardstick over and over again.

About a week later, the issue of wheels arose again. "Make wheels, Grandma." I found pan lids, paper plates, and Styrofoam plates thinking he might select one or the other for the wheels. He took a Styrofoam plate and held it on the bus. I gave him some Scotch tape, but he was unable to make the wheel stick. Next we tried masking tape. He was trying to put the plate onto the cardboard so that the curved side of the plate was next to the cardboard. Then I punched a hole in the plate and gave him a brad. He tried to put the brad through the hole but became frustrated. By then he was angry and beginning to cry, so I took some flimsy paper plates, punched holes in them, and attached them with brads to the box.

We used a luncheon plate for the steering wheel. Atticus took off this steering wheel time and time again. He tried and tried to reattach it, putting the brad into the plate, but he could not get the brad through the hole on the cardboard box. He also removed the windshield wiper over and over but was always unable to reattach it in spite of yards and yards of duct tape!

We stopped at a nearby bus company where we looked at the large and small school buses. Atticus was very hesitant to get close to any of the buses so we kept our distance. We did talk with the owner/dispatcher and asked for magazines that had pictures of buses. I went back to the bus company a week later and picked up the magazines. Atticus wasn't very interested in looking through the magazines, so I cut out several of the bus pictures and used them to make a bus book.

Each day when Atticus arrived, he would ask one of us to get the cardboard box bus out. We stored it on end in front of the closet. Once it was set on the floor, he would drag it over to an open space and climb in. Sometimes he "drove" the bus. Once he took his broom and swept out the inside of the bus. Then he took the dustpan and attempted to collect the dirt as he had seen me do many times in the kitchen.

One afternoon just before he lay down to take a nap, he tried to drag a sleeping bag into the bus. When I put the bag inside the bus, the entire floor was covered. Atticus found two stuffed animals, a rabbit and a gorilla, and put them inside. Then he drove the bus the rest of that day with the animals as passengers.

I found a video that contained the song "The Horn on the Bus." We played that section of the video every day for a week or so. No matter what Atticus was doing, he would stop and run over to stand near the television to watch. Sometimes he would sing along.

One day Atticus took his toy hammer and hammered on the bus. I cautioned him that too much hammering would make the bus break. He said, "I working, Grandma. I working." That day a breakable cup surrounded by six inches of Styrofoam arrived in the mail. Atticus took the Styrofoam cube and asked for tape. I gave him a long piece of duct tape, and he attempted to attach the cube to the back of the bus. I held the cube and tried to assist him by guiding the tape as he pressed it down. After four strips of tape, we managed to attach it to the bus. The gas tank!

The next day we stopped for gas on the way home from school. I took Atticus out of his car seat so that he could stand by the window and watch me get the gas. When we arrived back at the house, he found a plastic baseball bat and used it to put gas into the bus. From that day on, he always used the bat when filling up the gas tank.

We moved the bus into the kitchen in order to paint it. Atticus pulled off two wheels and put some paint on each one. Then he worked on the side of the bus. In all, he painted for about ten minutes. I tried to bring him back to the painting several times that day and again on another day the next week. He showed no interest in painting and didn't respond when I began to paint. Apparently, he didn't need to paint the box yellow to help him perceive the cardboard box as a bus.

Mary Ann made a memory book using some of the photos taken during the bus project. This page is one of many in the memory book.

PHASE THREE

I decided that the culminating experience would be sharing the information about the bus with Atticus's parents and his aunt and uncle. On a Friday night after school, we all gathered around the bus. As I pointed to things on the bus, Atticus said what they were. He showed everyone how to drive the bus. He filled the gas tank. He took off the steering wheel—again! By then he had discovered that you could put a key into the fold where the flaps of the box overlapped and that became the ignition switch. He used his set of keys to start the bus.

I took the bus pictures that we had used for reference and made them into a book for Atticus while he continued to play in the bus for another month. When I took the bus to school for the Parents' Sharing night, he noticed it was gone but did not ask about it again. The Bus Project was over.

As a culminating experience for the Bus Project, Atticus explained to his dad and aunt and uncle how the bus was made. In this photo, Atticus is showing his dad how to remove the windshield wiper.

As I reflect back on the Bus Project, I realize how powerful this learning experience was. Atticus was able to make decisions about the construction, and I became his hands. A toddler could not create a bus by himself. Atticus was able to use materials I supplied for parts of the bus. He found the windshield wiper and the gas tank by himself, showing that he was able to create on his own. We took many bus trips together, and he traveled with his animals. The opportunity to use imaginary play is so important in the lives of young children. Atticus worked on his bus and played with it. Our field experiences helped support his learning. His mom and dad were able to talk about his play and watch him engage in it. His knowledge of and vocabulary about buses were expanded because of this project.

I put together a collection of pictures from the project with comments for Atticus to have as a memory book. I included a page entitled "Grandma Reflects." Someday he will be able to read about this project and, hopefully, recall pleasant memories.

Would I do it again? Yes. In fact, Atticus is especially interested in the dirt outside ("Soil, Grandma"). We are already looking for worms.

EIGHT

Coaching Your Child

Although you may have begun parenthood with an image of your child as a ball of clay that you would mold and shape into your own image, we imagine that it was not too long before that changed. You began to realize that your child has a mind of his own and a process of growth that is not always easily controlled or directed. However, as we pointed out in Chapter 7, you have enormous impact on your child's development because you control in many ways the experiences your child has and the environment in which he exists. Part of that environment is created through the interactions (questions, smiles, directions, pats on the back, and so forth) that are directed to your child. Teachers go through this same process. However, the trained teacher usually has more goals in mind than a parent has and is consciously "coaching" the child toward these goals.

Understanding the Coaching Process

There are a few principles about the coaching process that may be helpful to you in many contexts as you interact with your child over the coming years.

1. Your child will develop skills at a pace similar to other children but with her own individuality. It is important to be flexible in your expectations.
2. Not all skills are appropriate to teach; your child must be ready for the skill physically and mentally. For example, trying to teach a 2-year-olds to read is not productive; in a few years it can be accomplished easily.
3. Most skills are learned step-by-step with each step building on the previous one.
4. You can support you child's acquisition of skills and her development by providing motivation and opportunities to practice.

A good analogy for the role that you can play in the development of your child is the role of a coach. You probably have had some experience with coaching, either being coached to learn a skill or having assisted another's learning. How does coaching work? If a baseball coach is helping a player learn how to bat, he will take the skill (batting) and break it down into parts, such as holding the bat, swinging, keeping your eye on the ball, and following through. As the coach works with the batter, he will often think of these smaller steps as a series of skills that build from basic to more advanced. He will figure out which of these skills he needs to support or teach by carefully observing the batter. Typically, he will first check how the batter holds the bat. If the batter is not holding the bat the way the coach thinks is most effective, he will show the batter the proper grip. Then he may concentrate his observations on how the batter swings, and so forth. The coach will communicate with the batter by observing carefully and then giving the batter just enough information that he can absorb and then make a simple alteration. The coach will encourage that change. A good coach knows that too many requests for change can be overwhelming and that positive reinforcement and appreciation maintain the batter's enthusiasm for baseball.

Many skills such as reading, writing, and math develop in the same way in children. As in baseball, some children receive the benefit of excellent coaching; others get little or poor coaching. As teachers, we can always tell when a child is receiving good coaching at home! Project work provides an excellent opportunity to provide coaching in many important areas of development, including school skills. In project work, children are drawing, reading, writing, counting, graphing, and building. There are many opportunities for children to become highly motivated to improve in these areas, and a project can provide a context for excellent coaching, which might not occur except in a homework situation.

Coaching General Project Skills

As you may have already figured out from reading the preceding chapters, there are a number of general skills that your child will use in project work. You may need to guide your child in the use of tools and techniques, communication, and planning and organizing. Continuing with the example of the baseball coach, let's explore each of these general skills in relation to how you will coach your player in the "project" game.

USE OF TOOLS AND TECHNIQUES

We begin with the use of tools. Tools in project work could include things like scissors, a screwdriver, wire cutters, or a number of other items that will assist you and your child as you work on your project. Part of the baseball coach's role is to show the player how to use a baseball bat. He might demonstrate how to hold a bat and even grasp the player from behind as the player practices swinging. However, when it is time to bat in the real game, the coach will stay on the sidelines and offer only verbal encouragement and advice. This is true for the parent coach as well. Take the use of scissors, for example. You might demonstrate how to hold scissors to cut paper and even cover your child's hand with your own as he cuts. At some point, however, your child will need to use the scissors independently. As the parent coach, it might be frustrating and difficult to watch as your child struggles, but you must be patient as he gains and develops new skills.

Like the use of tools, as the parent coach you will need to model some techniques. These could be skills such as how to work with modeling clay or how to use a hammer to pound a nail into wood. Similar to the use of tools, you will probably want to follow a sequence of demonstration, assistance, and finally independent use as your child develops the skill. Naturally, safety must be considered; you will never allow your child to independently use something like a circular saw no matter how proficient he might think he is! However, with practice and supervision, your child may be able to operate a cordless screwdriver with a minimum amount of help. Your child's experience, age, and abilities and your comfort level will all factor in to what will be appropriate for you and your child during project work. If you have a toddler, then your project experiences will be very different than if you have a school-age child. Watch for your child's nonverbal communication, such as gestures and facial expressions. These are clues to your child's abilities and understanding.

COMMUNICATION SKILLS

Projects also provide an opportunity for you to coach your child in the important skill of communicating with others. As you move through the project, there will be many opportunities for you to demonstrate verbal communication skills for your child. Often children know what they would like to say but lack the words to concisely and clearly verbalize what they are thinking. After allowing your child to share his thoughts with you, you might want to say something like, "So what you are saying (or wanting) is. . . ."

During Phase One of the Ball Project, Katie and her mom played with balls. There were many conversations in which mother gave words to Katie such as "Big ball!" This process continues as children grow.

Using verbal and nonverbal communication, Nanette explained and demonstrated how an airplane would look as it flew to countries on her map.

This allows you and your child to be clear and helps prevent frustrations from misunderstandings. As you talk with your child during project work, it is easy to tell her what to think or do, but this is where your patience can help your child come to her own discoveries and understandings. In project work, you want to support and foster independence, but you must allow time and opportunities for these skills to develop. You will also be modeling communication skills as you ask a librarian a question or as you call your uncle to see if he can serve as an expert for your topic. We know that children are very observant of our behavior, and modeling communication provides scripts and clues for children to use long after their early childhood years.

PLANNING AND ORGANIZING

As you organize materials and prepare for project work, you and your child will see the benefits of planning and thinking ahead. There are many tasks a baseball coach must complete before the team has a first practice. He has to obtain equipment, create practice schedules, and reserve a playing field. In the same way, you will need to make sure the project environment is ready:

- Did you get the clay your child will need to model?
- Is the morning clear of appointments so you and your child will have a block of time to work?
- Did you call the bakery to see if you could come and watch a cake being decorated?

These details can make or break the project work experience for you and your child. Like running out of an ingredient as you cook, minor details can ruin an

Elizabeth used her knowledge of letters and sounds to write a cookbook during her family's Cooking Project.

experience if you do not think ahead. As an adult, you know the frustrations that these mishaps cause. Your child will have similar feelings if he is excited about his work and cannot complete it.

Planning ahead, organizing materials, and preparing the environment will ensure that the project will go smoothly. While you are planning, organizing, and preparing for project work, you are also modeling these processes for your child. These skills will be of great benefit as she grows older and the projects change to things like homework and science fair projects.

Another opportunity for modeling occurs when the project does not proceed as planned and you have to be flexible and creative. For example, "The man we wanted to talk to isn't here today, but we could see if someone else could answer our questions." Being prepared and planning what you will do will help make the inevitable surprise or challenge more manageable. As anyone who spends time with children knows, surprises and unexpected events are commonplace. When the project does flow as planned, you can point this out to your child: "I'm glad we made a list of what you wanted to know. We didn't forget any of your questions!"

Coaching Representational Skills

As we described in Chapter 5, when your child is actively involved in meaningful learning, he has many different ways, or many different languages, to tell you about what he learned. Parents support children's representations of learning throughout childhood. Representation begins in play as a toddler picks up a banana, puts it to his ear, and talks into it like a telephone. It continues to develop, with the ultimate representation being the ability to pick up a pen, make marks on a paper, and communicate complex thoughts to another person.

Representation develops intellectual capacity. It is not simply a way to show thought; in the process of representing, significant thinking occurs. As an adult you have probably had the experience of not understanding a concept or a plan until you grabbed a pen and diagrammed it or drew a picture. The act of representing clarifies our understanding and enables us to see connections. This happens with the young child as he looks at a truck and attempts to draw a wheel or changes his voice and puts on pretend clothes to play a truck driver. Although pretending in play, drawing a picture, building a model, and writing may all seem like disconnected skills, in fact, they are all related. Experiences involving each of these activities enhance abilities to do the others. You can help your child develop representation skills through project work.

PRETEND PLAY

Play skills are developmental. This means that to a certain extent they are dependent on the age or the maturation of the child. However, play skills are also very responsive to the environment and the amount of time children have had to play. Typical development of play skills is shown in the chart at right. Parents can support children's play by providing time, opportunity, and encouragement for children to do pretend play. Recognize that play is your child's work, admire it, and focus on it. Don't hesitate to get involved!

Pretend play can be an important way for your child to represent learning in a project. As pointed out in Chapter 5, you can collect artifacts related to the project to enable pretend play and construction of a play environment in your home. When your child is building a play structure, listen to what she says about the structure. If you recognize what she has represented, let her know by saying something like, "I see you have a place for the people who come to the orchard to park." Ask questions that will enable your child to talk about structures: "Where will you keep the apples cold?" Examine photos and drawings that your child has made of a field site to see if there is additional work that she would like to do.

You can let your child know that you value his play by getting down on the floor and joining pretend play. "Can I be an apple picker too? I will take this basket here." "I'll be a customer in your pizza shop." You can extend your child's play, which will lead to development of a longer attention span. When your child appears to run out of ideas, introduce an addition he can make to his structure or a new role that can be added to a play event. Above all, recognize and encourage your child when he spends time in productive play. "You played for a long time with your apple orchard." "You worked very hard to make that ramp for the trucks just right!"

DRAWING AND PAINTING

The effect of coaching and support is most evident in drawing and painting during project work. Young children use drawing to take notes on field-site visits. They use drawing and painting to "sort out" what they know about objects and relationships.

Drawing is also developmental; that is, as shown in the chart on page 124, to a certain extent maturation is required for the skill to develop. We do not expect

Representation Through Play

Representation Through	What It Looks Like	Typical Progress
Imitation with objects	Child uses objects to pretend Begins about 12 months and extends through elementary school	First, uses real objects to pretend, then uses substitute objects like blocks, then can pretend without any objects Short play events of a few minutes
Make believe play	Begins with child playing with toys and pretending they are real, making noises as a toddler Ages 3 to 4 child dresses up and pretends to "be" someone	First, acts out play without words and by self (such as running a toy truck), then uses words and talks like the person the child is pretending to be May play in this way for a period of time, usually less than 10 minutes
Dramatic play with others	Ages 4, 5, and up develop extensive play episodes with complex roles	Involves others in play, talking, dressing, and acting in role Play episodes last 10 minutes or longer

Information from *Pathways to Play: Developing Play Skills in Young Children* by Sandra Heidemann and Deborah Hewitt, Redleaf Press (1992); *The Creative Curriculum for Preschool* by Diane Trister Dodge, Laura J. Colker, Cate Heroman, and Toni S. Bickart, Teaching Strategies; 4th edition (2002); *The Effects of Sociodramatic Play on Disadvantaged Preschool Children* by Sara Smilansky, Wiley, (1968).

toddlers to be able to hold a pencil and draw like a 5-year-old. However, drawing is also developed through practice and encouragement. To encourage drawing and painting as representational skills, you can model them. This can be done by sketching alongside your child at field-site visits and also when you return home. If drawing and painting materials are easily accessible, as described in Chapter 2, your child is more likely to use these forms of representation.

If your child has difficulty beginning to draw, you might try this advice from the Drawing Study Group:

- Ask questions that focus your child on the topic.
- Ask questions that uncover what your child knows: "What is this called? What is it used for?"
- Ask questions to help your child make associations, to clarify ideas, and to create enthusiasm for the task: "How are the wheels the same and different? Which part helps you steer?"
- Ask questions that help your child visualize a phenomenon.
- Ask questions to help your child figure out how to translate responses into marks and lines on paper: "Which parts are connected to the big wheel? How will you draw their shapes?"
- Ask questions that can help your child make the transition from looking to getting started drawing: "Which part will you draw first? How will you connect this part?"

Representation Through Art

Representation Through	What It Looks Like	Typical Progress
Disordered scribbling	Random scribbles in many directions	Typical of 2-year-olds
		They may pretend to draw just at they would pretend to read by holding a book and doing the motions
Controlled scribbling	Scribbles have direction and shape	Typical of older 2-year-olds and some 3-year-olds
		Again, the act of drawing or painting is what is important; it is not likely to be representational
Naming a picture that was not planned	Children will make lines or shapes and then will often relate that to a current interest	Many 3-year-olds will draw and then relate their drawing to the project topic
Drawing	Drawing is deliberate looking at the object and drawing, or drawing later from memory	At about age 4 children become aware of their ability to create an image that is related to their topic of study
	Products are recognizable	They will continue to work on their ability to do this throughout the elementary grades

Summarized from *The Creative Curriculum for Early Childhood* by Diane Trister Dodge, Teaching Strategies (1989).

It also may be helpful to draw your child's attention to her paper and get started on actually drawing by asking, "Where will you draw (whatever it is your child has selected to draw)? Can you put your pencil where you are going to start drawing?" If you are drawing next to your child, you can think aloud about your own drawing. Do not show your child exactly how to draw the item or do it for her. Remember that your role is to coach.

Coaching Reading and Writing

Helping your child become a confident and independent reader and writer is one of the most important jobs you can undertake. Project work is a wonderful way to encourage the skills of reading and writing and to support your child as he makes sense of the written word.

Remember that you are your child's model for a reader/writer. Think about your own reading habits.

- Do you read where your child can see you?
- Is the TV off when you are reading?
- Do you make time every night to read with your child?
- Does your child observe you reading to find answers (reading the label on a medicine bottle, using the telephone book, reading directions for a toy)?

Learning to Write

Scribble Writing	~~⌇⌇⌇⌇~~
Letter-Like Shapes	D X LO(MM)
Stringing Letters	T BRSCL
Writing Consonants	J W T G T P (I want to go to the park)
Phonetic Spelling	Luk fr mi blks plez (Look for my blocks please)
Conventional Spelling	Can I have a cookie?

Information from *Learning to Read and Write: Developmentally Appropriate Practice for Young Children* by Neuman, Copple, and Bredekamp. NAEYC. (1999); *Teaching Kids to Spell* by Gentry and Gillet. Heinemann. (1993).

Parents who read usually have children who read. As your child watches you read, she will often ask the first questions about the reading process: "What does that say? What is that word?" The learning-to-read process has begun!

When you think about reading and writing as a part of everything you do, the opportunities to engage your child in literacy activities will happen almost automatically. You do not have to isolate moments for reading and writing—it does not have to become so school-like! When your child is drawing a picture of something in your project, such as a tree, ask him if he would like to write the word *tree* on his drawing. If he says, "I don't know how," offer to write it on your paper. Say, "This is how I would write *tree* on my paper." Usually, a child will attempt to write the word. Accept his writing according to whatever stage of writing development he is in. Writing, just like walking and talking, has definite stages, and your child will probably experience most of them. The chart on this page shows the stages of writing development. In the classroom, we usually begin talking to children about writing words when they are about 3 and a half years old.

Similarly, at about the same age we begin to model how a book is used and how reading occurs by making comments like, "I have to start at the top of the page because that's where the words start." Pointing out parts of the book is important too, like the front and back of the book, title page, and author's name. You will often need to stimulate your child's interest in words by making it more meaningful to them personally, like "Look! That butterfly word starts with the same letter as your name! BBBonnie and BBButterfly have the same first letter!" Soon your child will be looking for words that begin with the same letter as her name.

It is important to think of your child as a reader and writer from day one and unconditionally accept his first attempts at reading a book or writing a sign. For example, say things like, "You're right, that is a B word. It says butterfly. Look at the picture, and it will give you a clue about the words on the page," or "Tell me what your writing says (it might be some scribbles). Let me show you how I would write that." This type of parent coaching will empower your child immediately and encourage further attempts.

When children are encouraged to put their thoughts down on paper without the stress of worrying about correct spelling or correct letter formation, they quickly come to think of themselves as real writers and that writing has a purpose. When your child is engaged in project work and representing what she is learning, she will understand that writing conveys meaning and she is not just "practicing her letters."

Writing experiences can be incorporated into almost every aspect of project work. When your child is drawing, very often he will want to tell you about his picture. This is the point when you as the project partner can suggest that he label

Caleb was encouraged by his mother to write the word snake on his drawing of the black snake at the pet store.

his drawing. Using a technique called guided writing, ask your child to listen for the first letter in the word and then to write it beside his drawing. You can continue to do this for each letter, watching for frustration to set in. When it does, finish writing the words for him, modeling conventional writing. Using this guided writing technique, you and your child can

Label drawings
Collect and display new words learned
Make signs for construction
Make books about what you are learning
Draw and label maps
Keep observation records
Make a picture/project word dictionary
List items needed for construction

School-age children who are already readers and writers can incorporate literacy into every aspect of project work. At this level, children could keep journals of their day-to-day progress during the project. With encouragement, they could write short stories about their topic or keep a dictionary of the new words they have learned during the investigations. These older children could write and illustrate their own books about the project topic as a part of the celebration activities at the end of the project. With school-age children, the possibilities are endless, and your most important consideration is whether you have enough paper and pencils! Of course, school-age children are also very capable of using a word processor on the computer. They will enjoy using more technical equipment to document their learning.

The reading process, just like the writing process, has definite stages that your child will go through on her way to becoming a confident reader. (The chart on the next page shows the stages of reading development.) Just as you encourage your child's first writing attempts, it is important to accept her first reading attempts.

While reading to your child, you can help him understand many features of print, including that the words carry the meaning (not the pictures), that a string of letters is a word, that our eyes move left to right when we read, and that reading progresses top to bottom. When you, as the project partner, demonstrate how print works, your child will develop critical concepts such as word awareness. When using a book with your child, first read through the book once, helping her become

"Backhoe Loader"

Four-year-old Luke wrote the words backhoe loader *during a project on construction. It was his first attempt at connecting sounds with letters he knew to make a word.*

Learning to Read

Recognizing environmental print	Your child will see the big M on the "Golden Arches" and shout "That says McDonalds!"
Making an association between written and spoken language	Your child will begin to understand that the words she sees in the book are the words you're reading to her.
Recognizing the first letter in his name	Your child will identify and shout out whenever he sees the letter that begins his name, "Look! McDonald's has an M just like in my name, Michael!"
Recognizing her name and the names of her friends	Your child will recognize her name and the names of her favorite friends.
Associating sound with the corresponding letters	Your child will begin to hear the sounds the letters make and say things like, "A letter B says BBB."
Hearing and identifying words that rhyme	Your child will begin to interrupt you when you're reading saying, "Hey! Bat and cat sound the same!"
Recognizing familiar words out of context	Your child will begin to recognize words that she sees and hears a lot, like cat, run, look, the, said, and it. These are called *high frequency words*.
Attempting to sound out words	Your child will begin to sound out words while using the illustrations for clues as to what the text says.
Increasing fluency	Once your child begins to read, she will read the same books over and over again, increasing her fluency and building her confidence.

Summarized from *Learning to Read and Write: Developmentally Appropriate Practice for Young Children* by Newman, Copple, and Bredekamp, NAEYC (1999); *Teaching Kids to Read and Write* by Gentry and Gillet, Heinemann (1993).

familiar with the rhythm and pattern of the book. During the second or third reading (because every child chants, "Read it one more time!"), begin to point out some words that are repeated or letters that dominate a page. For example, when reading a book like *Things That Fly,* point out all the words that begin with the letter *B:* "Oh look! bat, butterfly, and bird all start with the letter B and they all make that B-B-B sound. Can you find anymore?" This type of "shared reading" experience enhances children's exposure to and understanding of the written word. Encouraging your child to remember story sequence and information from the book will get them excited about the reading process, and soon they will be telling you, "I can read this book all by myself!"

The school-age child who is already a reader should be encouraged to seek answers through reading reference books. You can model this research process by saying, "I don't know the answer. Have you looked in all the library books?" Supporting your older child by sitting with him and helping him read the information from the more difficult reference books will encourage him to use reference books in future projects. Your school-age child, depending on his age, is moving toward becoming an independent reader. Make sure some of the books you choose for your project will allow your child to read information on his own. Planning a time for reading within your family project time is important. Sometimes the project work for that day could begin with the project books. That short reading time could direct the project activities for that day or in some cases determine the direction a project takes.

When children feel empowered as readers and writers, their project representations become powerful documentations of their learning. Project work offers many opportunities for you and your child to share in her development into a lifelong reader and writer.

Coaching Mathematical Development

As project work develops, many math skills will become necessary when constructions begin or even in the collection of materials. While the need for your child to count and measure seems obvious, many more math concepts might be developed and used during the project. In early childhood, children are developing many problem-solving skills and new approaches to mathematical thinking. Your child should develop general as well as specific math skills. Young children will begin to learn about numbers and operations such as adding. A benefit of project work is the way that children can

Caleb uses a ruler to measure a worm during the Slime Project.

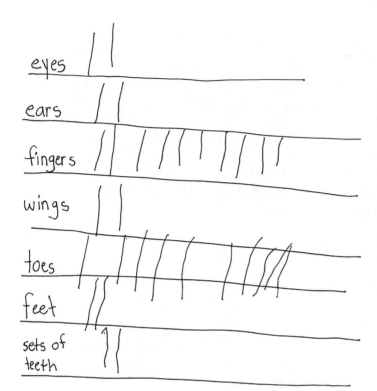

eyes

ears

fingers

wings

toes

feet

sets of
teeth

Four-year-old Aimee used her developing math skills to make this tally chart of the parts of a bat during the Bat Project.

develop an understanding of when to apply math principles. You can help your child develop strategies when encountering mathematical problems. When children experience math in a practical way, they are more appreciative of learning and understanding math as a useful skill.

The chart on the following page traces the development of a number of broad mathematical skills and how children progress through each level. As with all areas of development, children pass through these levels at varying paces. While the chart lists specific skills children develop, your child's attitude toward math can be greatly enhanced by experiences you provide through project work. You can use the chart to gauge which skills your child has and how you might help your child learn new skills. This chart can help you to meet your child at her developmental level and then encourage her to progress toward the next area of development. Information about development can be especially helpful when children's work is beyond the typical age expectations, as in a seriated ball sequence produced by a 2-year-old in the Ball Project.

Keeping the Project Fun

Although there are many advantages to incorporating school skills and challenging your child to think during project work, we feel that it is very important to

Learning to Think Mathematically

Mathematical Skill	What It Looks Like	Typical Progress
Sorting	Sorts and groups objects by color, size, shape, use, etc.	2-year-olds sort by color (such as M&Ms), then 3- to 4-year-olds sort by color, size, shape (such as sorting blocks), then kindergarteners and older children sort by use, categories such as zoo animals/farm animals
Patterning	Recognizes, copies, and makes up patterns	4-year-olds recognize patterns such as girl/boy/girl/boy in a line, then 4- and 5-year-olds will copy a pattern (such as the way beads alternate in a necklace), then kindergarten children will make up their own patterns
Number Concepts	Shows interest in counting and numbers	3-year-olds match numbers of items (such as one plate for each person), then 3- and 4-year-olds can count meaningfully about five objects, then kindergarteners count meaningfully to 20 and know that numbers indicate less and more, then primary-school-age children use numbers to solve problems
Geometry	Identifies and labels several shapes	3-year-olds match shapes, then 4-year-olds identify shapes by name, then kindergarteners can create shapes, then primary-school-age children can solve problems and puzzles with shapes
Measurement	Measures	3- and 4-year-olds use words to compare (such as big:little, short:long), then 4-year-olds begin to use non-standard ways to measure (such as measuring an object using blocks or scales that balance), then kindergarteners begin to use standard tools to measure (such as rulers, yardsticks, scales with numbers), then primary-school-age children use more complex tools (such as meter sticks, scales with numbers) to solve problems
Time	Develops a sense of time	3-year-olds develop a sense of today, tomorrow, past, and future, then 4-year-olds begin to attach meaning to specific days (like church day), then kindergarteners understand the days of the week and months, then primary-school-age children understand years, seasons, and that historical events happened a long time ago

This information is summarized from *The Omnibus Guidelines: Preschool Through Third Grade* by Judy R. Jablon, Dorothea B. Marsden, Samuel J. Meisels, and Margo Dichtelmiller, Rebus and Associates (1994).

Although charts of typical development are helpful, your child's development may not match the charts. This seriation (putting objects in line from smallest to largest) was done by a 2-year-old in the Ball Project.

remember that this is a fun activity that you are doing with your child. If the project becomes too "school-like," your child might be turned off, thinking that you are doing the project only because you want him to do more "homework." This is not the purpose of project work within the family. Projects are intended to be a shared, interesting experience. Remember to have fun together and enjoy each other's company. This is perhaps the greatest of all the benefits of project work for both you and your child.

NINE

Adapting the Project Approach to Specific Situations

Going beyond the basics of the project approach described in Part II of this book, in this chapter we want to answer questions about how to use project work in family child care, in home schooling, and with gifted children.

How Can a Family Child Care Provider Incorporate the Project Approach into Daily Activities?

Organization and creativity are the answers to this question! By spending entire days with children, you, as a family child care provider, can see what type of topics and activities really interest individual children. Depending on your situation, you might choose to focus on one child's interest and then try to engage some other children in the group. You will probably find it easiest if one project is occurring at a time. By choosing quality topics to explore, all children in the group can benefit. When choosing a topic, ideas can come from home and around the neighborhood. Topics from nature—plants, birds, trees—lend themselves to project work, as do things such as balls, shoes, and other common items in the home.

With a group of children of varying ages, you might want to plan activities during the rest time of little ones so the older children can focus on their project work. For site visits, you might want to arrange for extra help so the older children involved in the project can ask questions and do field sketches. Perhaps having an expert come into your home and share information might be easier for the group. The topic and ages of the children will have a great impact on how the project work will best be completed.

Within your home children will need access to materials. These can be stored in large Rubbermaid tubs that can be stacked when children leave. Poster boards are also great ways to display work, and they can be put away and protected from smaller children. Chapter 2 discusses ways to provide materials in an organized manner. The most important aspect of project work is that you create an environment and provide opportunities for children of all ages to engage in activities that promote meaningful learning.

As you work through the various aspects of project work—topic, environment, experts—refer to the Family Project Planning Journal at the back of the book. It provides a detailed outline that will assist you and help you get organized as you think through a specific project.

How Can the Project Approach Be Used in Home Schooling?

We feel that project work is a natural match for the home-schooling process. Project work can provide a way to follow children's interests and passions. As children become accustomed to following the project approach structure, they should be able to provide a structure to their own learning. We have seen this happen in classrooms where children have had extensive experience with project work. We have had children identify a topic and then say, "Ok, let's get out the paper and make a web of what we know! Then we will make up our questions!" Project work can provide a motivation for learning academic skills and also provide a way to practice these skills.

It might be helpful for you as a home-schooling parent to think of knowledge and skills that you want your child to learn on a continuum, similar to the way classroom teachers approach project work. The chart on this page shows a variety of approaches to teaching knowledge and skills to children on a continuum of the amount of child determination or what we call *child initiation* in the learning experience.

Degree of Child Initiation and Decision Making in Different Approaches to Teaching

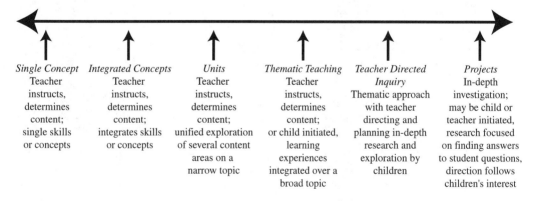

Single Concept	*Integrated Concepts*	*Units*	*Thematic Teaching*	*Teacher Directed Inquiry*	*Projects*
Teacher instructs, determines content; single skills or concepts	Teacher instructs, determines content; integrates skills or concepts	Teacher instructs, determines content; unified exploration of several content areas on a narrow topic	Teacher instructs, determines content; or child initiated, learning experiences integrated over a broad topic	Thematic approach with teacher directing and planning in-depth research and exploration by children	In-depth investigation; may be child or teacher initiated, research focused on finding answers to student questions, direction follows children's interest

Less child initiation and decision making

More child initiation and decision making

From *Young Investigators: The Project Approach in the Early Years* by Judy Harris Helm and Lilian Katz, Teachers College Press (2001), p. 20.

All experiences on the continuum are good ways to learn. Not all knowledge and skills that children need to learn are most easily taught through project work or are child-initiated learning experiences. There are many things that are unlikely to be initiated by children that we must make sure they learn (such as learning how to cross a street safely). These are easier for children to learn if they are told the information or shown the skill. Other skills and knowledge are learned best by reading from a number of sources. Still others require direct, systematic instruction and practice. As we work with children as parents or as teachers, we find that the amount of child initiation in the learning process is often directly related to the nature of the knowledge or skills we want children to learn. For example, the Oregon Trail may be taught easily as a unit, but pond animals can be an exciting child-directed project.

We believe that in home schooling, the flexibility of the curriculum and the small number of children means that project work could become a significant part of children's learning experiences. We also feel that project work is probably not going to provide all of the experiences that children need to develop their knowledge, skills, and dispositions. However, if the learning experiences that children have fall mainly on the left side of the continuum with very little on the right, children's dispositions to be curious, engaged learners will be damaged.

The home-schooling parent will probably find books and resources on the project approach designed for classroom teachers to be helpful in home schooling because they provide guidance in how to incorporate academic skills such as math, reading, science inquiry, and the arts. One of the techniques is the use of an instructional planning web, such as the one shown on the next page.

This web shows how Pam and her coteacher Lora thought carefully about where academic skills might emerge and where they might be practiced in the project process. An anticipatory planning web can enable you to pinpoint opportunities for meeting standards or covering required curriculum during project work. The technique of webbing is described fully in *Young Investigators,* and you are strongly encouraged to use it as a supplement to this book, even if you are home schooling children who are proficient readers and writers. You can find out more information in the Resources for Further Reading at the back of the book.

How Can the Project Approach Be Used with Gifted Children?

We feel that the project approach can be especially helpful for parents of gifted children. Our combined experiences with gifted children include directing a university program, teaching in a program for gifted children, and also parenting gifted children. We found projects to be a wonderful way to support gifted children's learning. Projects enable children to study interests that are not "typical" of children their age. For example, at the age of 5, one of our children was very interested in the life and times of Abraham Lincoln. This lead to a project on Abraham Lincoln that lasted for several months, including visits to New Salem, where Lincoln had lived

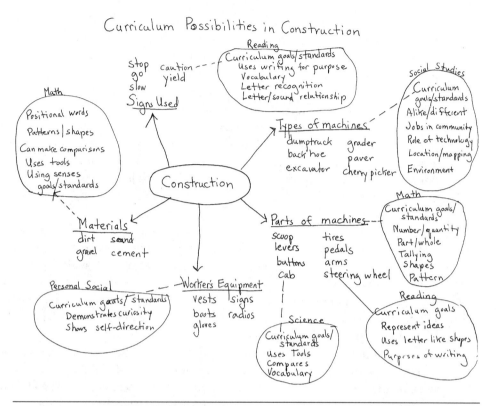

Curriculum Possibilities in Construction

This anticipatory planning web was completed by Pam before the Construction Project began. It enabled the anticipation of opportunities to integrate curriculum goals.

and where she talked to the interpreters in the log cabins. She read many books and engaged in extensive dramatic play centered on Abraham Lincoln.

There are many recommended learning experiences in project work that are naturally compatible with recommendations for experiences for gifted children. Some of these include the following:

1. *Learning can move from concrete experiences to abstract thinking.* The collection of artifacts and visiting of field sites assure that children get lots of hands-on, concrete experiences. As a parent, encouraging your child to talk, write, and draw about what she is learning helps her take those concrete experiences and move into abstract thinking.

2. *Learning can be pitched slightly above the child's level of performance.* Because project work in the home occurs individually, you can help your child learn and practice math skills, writing skills, and problem solving at a level appropriate for him, regardless of his age or typical grade-level curriculum.

3. *Opportunities can be provided for real life applications and creative responses.* Projects at home can involve meaningful applications of many skills that your child is

learning in and out of school. Your child can draw, color, paint, build, construct, create music, and write about the project topic. She can come up with ideas to share what she has learned, such as making posters. Projects can also result in service to the community.

4. *Experiences can provide greater complexity and challenge.* In project work at home, you can go into the topic in as much depth as your child wants. For example, a young child might learn about how the motor turns wheels in a car and how a transmission works.

5. *Projects can provide opportunities for critical and creative thinking.* In project work, there are many opportunities for your child to identify and solve his own problems. Your child often has to come up with solutions such as how to make part of a model stand up or how to design a part of a machine. In project work, your child gets the opportunity to not only come up with ideas but to try them out. He learns to appreciate that there are many ways to do things and that he can make judgments about the best way to accomplish his goals.

6. *Projects emphasize an integrated framework for understanding.* When your child is working on projects, she can see the usefulness of certain skills and knowledge such as reading, writing, and using numbers. As she works on subsequent projects, she can see similarities in how these skills are used in each project. Subsequent projects will also allow her to see similar characteristics in such things as jobs that people do, uses of computers, or stores, regardless what they sell. Research skills developed in one project can be applied in another.

These suggestions are partly based on the work of Joyce Van-Tassel Baska, executive director of the Center for Gifted Education at the College of William and Mary.

In Closing

Now that you know a lot about project work and how it happens in families, we invite you to take the plunge. As we tell our parents, all you have to do is make up your mind to start. You can start big, or you can start small; you can jump into a big project or start with a mini-exploration. However, we urge you not to wait. We, as parents, are shocked at how little time we have in the long term with these wonderful, magical creatures that share our lives. Remember this is your child's only summer as a 3-year-old, or his only spring as a 5-year-old, or her only winter as an 8-year-old. And this is your only time to be a dad, a mom, a grandparent, or a special caregiver. Don't miss this precious opportunity to have an impact on the lives of the children who are so important to you. Remember, there are no project police! You can't do it wrong, but you can miss out on a wonderful opportunity to enjoy life and get to know your child. How can you get started today? Go to page 4 of the Family Project Planning Journal and discover what interests *your* child. A great adventure awaits you!

Glossary

anticipatory planning web   A web completed by a teacher anticipating how curriculum objectives can be integrated into a project. Used in classroom projects.

artifact   An object that your child collects and studies during project work. Artifacts include equipment (such as a tire pump), pieces of an item (such as the insides of a radio), clothing that adults use when working (such as an apron or a hat), and tools (such as a hammer).

coaching   Participating in the learning process and supporting your child as she problem solves, investigates, and represents what she is learning.

culminating activities or **culmination**   A variety of activities during Phase Three of a project in which you and your child summarize and explain your work and findings to others.

documentation   Processes of keeping records and samples of your child's work at different stages of the project, which reveal how your child worked and what learning occurred.

expert   Anyone who has knowledge about the project topic at a level higher than your child. It could be a family member, a neighbor, or someone in the community.

field-site visit   Planned visits to places where information can be obtained related to project work. Field-site visits usually include observation drawing, questioning of experts on site, photographing, and collecting artifacts.

guided writing   Modeling writing in front of your child. For example, when helping your child write a word, you would encourage him to write the letters he knows and then you would write the rest of the letters.

modeling   Demonstrating the behavior that you want your child to learn. For example, when encouraging problem solving, you might let your child see you fail and then think aloud about other possibilities to try. The adult "thinks out loud" so that the child will hear the problem-solving process.

observation drawing   Drawings and sketches made while looking at actual objects or places as a way to study and record what is observed.

one-to-one correspondence   The ability to match one object to another object such as one cup for each plate or one cookie for each child. One-to-one correspondence enables the child to say a numeral name for each object when counting.

problem solving   A way to find a solution by defining a problem, coming up with possible solutions, and then testing the solutions.

project   An extended, in-depth investigation of a topic. Projects involve your child in conducting research on phenomena or events worth learning about in his own environment.

project approach   An approach to teaching using projects that follows the structure of three phases of your child's investigation.

representation   An expression of a child's understanding of a topic by talking about it, drawing it, building it, making up songs or dances about it, or playing out experiences.

representations   Products of representation—a painting, a drawing, a dance.

shared reading   Involving your child in the reading process. For example, you could have your child repeat rhyming words, pause when she knows a phrase, or let her read the parts of the book that she knows.

Time 1/Time 2 documentation   Drawings, pictures, webs, or other representations collected during a project at sequential times. For example, this could be a web of what your child knows at the beginning of a project and a web at the end of the project; or a child's drawing of a fire truck after the first time he saw one and then a drawing done later after studying fire trucks.

web or **topic web**   A graphic representation of the ideas about a topic with the topic in the center and concepts related to the topic branching out from the center.

webbing   Discussing with your child what she knows or wants to know about a topic and recording it as a web.

Resources for Further Reading

Learning to Use the Project Approach

Helm, Judy Harris, & Katz, Lilian G. (2001). *Young Investigators: The Project Approach in the Early Years.* Early Childhood Education Series. Available from Teachers College Press, P.O. Box 20, Williston, VT 05495-0020. 145pp.

This step-by-step guide is designed to help teachers in doing projects with children who are not yet proficient at reading and writing. Each phase is described in detail with practical advice from teachers using the project approach in classrooms for toddlers through first grade. A Project Planning Journal at the end of the book guides teachers who are new to project work through the project process with checklists and reflection questions. The Journal can also be used for organizing documentation for those teachers more experienced with project work. The Fire Truck Project, which took place in a preschool classroom with children with special needs, is described in detail. An accompanying video, *A Children's Journey: The Fire Truck Project,* enables viewers to see the children involved in the project and hear the teacher describe the process of the project. The video is also available from Teachers College Press.

Katz, Lilian G., & Chard, Sylvia C. (2000). *Engaging Children's Minds: The Project Approach* (2nd Ed.). Available from Ablex Publishing Corp., P.O. Box 811, Stamford, CT 06904-0811. 215pp.

This latest edition of the classic description of the project approach by Katz and Chard presents the theoretical base of the project approach. Although written for teachers, the book provides an in-depth explanation of the reasons for including project work in children's lives that may be helpful to parents.

Chard, Sylvia C. (1998). *Project Approach: Developing the Basic Framework. Practical Guide 1; Project Approach: Developing Curriculum with Children. Practical Guide 2.* Available from Scholastic, Inc., 555 Broadway, New York, NY 10012. 64pp.

These guides are especially helpful for home schooling and for teachers of children who are old enough to independently use reading and writing as learning tools. The guides present many classroom ideas to support and integrate curriculum activities into project work. The three phases of project work are described fully, including teacher roles and student roles.

Child Development and Coaching

Meisels, Sam; Stetson, Charlotte, & Marsden, Dorothea. (2000). *Winning Ways to Learn: Ages 3, 4, 5; Winning Ways to Learn: Ages 6, 7, 8.* Available from Goddard Press, NY.

These books describe children's typical development in personal-social relations, language and literacy, mathematical thinking, scientific thinking, social studies, the arts, and physical development and health in a parent-friendly way. Parents can see if their children are on track and avoid either pushing them inappropriately or missing early signs of difficulty. They also provide many appropriate ways to painlessly integrate learning experiences into everyday life. There are many ideas to stimulate curiosity and interests, which might lead to good project work.

Burns, M. Susan, Snow; Catherine E., & Griffin, Peg Griffin (Editors). (1999). *Starting Out Right: A Guide to Promoting Children's Reading Success.* Available from National Academy Press.

A guide for parents and caregivers to beginning reading, this book provides many practical, hands-on activities and ideas for integrating reading into learning experiences. Milestones are provided for each age level so parents can know if their child is on track or not.

About the Authors

JUDY HARRIS HELM, ED.D., assists schools and early childhood programs in integrating research and new methods through her consulting and training company, Best Practices, Inc. She began her career teaching first grade then taught, directed, and designed early childhood and primary programs as well as trained teachers at the community college, undergraduate, and graduate levels. She served on the Task Force for the design of the Valeska Hinton Early Childhood Education Center, a state-of-the-art urban collaboration school for children age three through first grade in Peoria, Illinois, and then became Professional Development Coordinator for the school. She is past state president of the Illinois Association for the Education of Young Children. Dr. Helm is coauthor of *Windows on Learning: Documenting Children's Work, Teacher Materials for Documenting Children's Work,* and *Young Investigators: The Project Approach in the Early Years* and coeditor of *The Power of Projects.* She is the mother of Amanda and Rebecca, now grown, who thrived on project work.

STACY BERG is an early childhood educator and the director of Northminster Learning Center in Peoria, Illinois. In her current position she develops faith-based, developmentally appropriate programming for toddlers, preschoolers, and grade school children. Professionally, she enjoys consulting with teachers and programs and presenting to groups at conferences on supporting project work and faith-based education. Stacy is the mother of three children under the age of five—kindergartner Drew, preschooler Seth, and baby Jena—and does projects in her home.

PAM SCRANTON, B.S., a classroom teacher in Discovery Preschool, is in her eighteenth year as an early childhood educator. She is currently completing a master's program in curriculum and instruction. Pam taught at Valeska Hinton Early Childhood Education Center and in the Woodford County Special Education Bright Beginnings program before coming to the Northminster Learning Center to teach in the Discovery Preschool program. She is a frequent presenter in school districts on topics such as engaging children in project work, authentic assessment, and developmentally appropriate practice. She is a contributing author of *The Power of Projects.* Pam is the mother of teenager Lauren and two elementary school boys, Joey and Alex.

THE FAMILY PROJECT
PLANNING JOURNAL

This journal accompanies

Teaching Your Child to Love Learning:
A Guide to Doing Projects at Home

JUDY HARRIS HELM
STACY BERG
PAM SCRANTON

HOW TO RAISE CHILDREN
WHO LOVE TO LEARN

This journal is designed to be used with the chapters in this book, *Teaching Your Child to Love Learning: A Guide to Doing Projects at Home.* The purpose of the journal is to help you support your child's project work by providing a step-by-step review of the project approach and a place to draw-up plans and record results. This journal should be copied and inserted in a loose-leaf binder with pocket pages or scrapbook pages for collecting children's work.

THE PROJECT APPROACH

What is the project approach?

The project approach is an in-depth study of a particular topic by a child or group of children. The project approach structure was developed by Dr. Lilian Katz at the University of Illinois.

How is it different from others ways of learning?

In project work your child will study a topic of interest for a long time period. You will select a topic that your child is interested in and is meaningful to him in his life. Your child will go into great depth in his study and often at a level higher than many adults would expect for his age.

How will your child learn?

Your child will use a variety of ways to find answers to questions. These include traditional resources like books. Other resources usually include field-site visits and/or interviews with experts. An expert is anyone who knows a great deal about the topic. Your child will plan questions for interviews and have tasks to do on field-site visits. Your child may also make field notes and draw or write on-site. She may also make plans for building things and engage in pretend play about the topic, which helps her sort out what she is learning.

Your child will do problem solving with you structuring problems and assisting in finding solutions and resources. Your child will redraw and rewrite as more is learned. Some of the ways that children record their learning are project books, murals, artwork, constructions, and journals.

The Project Approach for Families

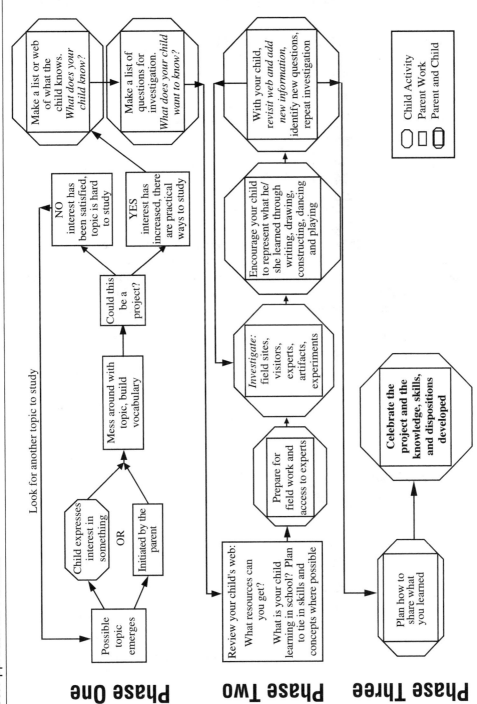

Phase One

Possible topic emerges

Child expresses interest in something OR Initiated by the parent

Look for another topic to study

Mess around with topic, build vocabulary

Could this be a project?

NO interest has been satisfied, topic is hard to study

YES interest has increased, there are practical ways to study

Make a list or web of what the child knows. *What does your child know?*

Make a list of questions for investigation. *What does your child want to know?*

Phase Two

Review your child's web: What resources can you get? What is your child learning in school? Plan to tie in skills and concepts where possible

Prepare for field work and access to experts

Investigate: field sites, visitors, experts, artifacts, experiments

Encourage your child to represent what he/she learned through writing, drawing, constructing, dancing and playing

With your child, *revisit web and add new information,* identify new questions, repeat investigation

Phase Three

Plan how to share what you learned

Celebrate the project and the knowledge, skills, and dispositions developed

Child Activity
Parent Work
Parent and Child

Phase One

GETTING STARTED WITH YOUR PROJECT

IDENTIFYING YOUR CHILD'S INTEREST

The project topic is determined by your child's interest. Projects can start in two ways:

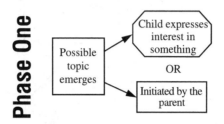

Young children (2–4 years) show you they are interested in a subject by

- Asking questions
- Requesting information
- Pushing forward to look at something
- Picking up items
- Hoarding "souvenirs"
- Focusing on things for a longer time than usual
- Attending carefully to what others say about a subject

School-age children (5 years and up) show they are interested by

- Asking questions (How does that work? What is that for? What does he do?)
- Asking for information
- Spending time examining items
- Saving items
- Starting collections
- Paying more attention to conversations about the topic
- Requesting to go places that relate to the topic (such as an airport)

Parent Journal: *What are some interests that I have observed in my child in the past?*

WHEN YOUR CHILD APPEARS TO HAVE AN INTEREST

If your child seems to be interested in something, like trucks, you can try out that topic as a project. Encourage your child to **think more** about it. *Mess around with the topic.* This provides background knowledge for both of you. For example, with the topic of trucks you could

With Younger Children
- Talk about trucks
- Read a book about trucks
- Play trucks together
- Help your child draw pictues of trucks
- Look at real trucks in parking lots, etc.
- Collect brochures, diagrams, photos
- Provide parts and pieces of real trucks

With Older Children
- Involve children in doing adult tasks related to trucks
- Provide parts and pieces of real trucks
- Provide access to real tools related to trucks
- Take children on a mini-field-site visit (for example to watch someone change oil)
- Provide nonfiction books about trucks
- Collect brochures, diagrams, and any print sources about trucks

If your child's curiosity is satisfied or if the child doesn't show much interest, look for another topic. If your child shows signs of still being interested, you may have a project!

WHEN YOUR CHILD DOESN'T APPEAR TO HAVE A PARTICULAR INTEREST

Children, even in primary school, don't always show interests on their own. Often a child may need to be encouraged to focus on something and to think about it so that an interest may develop. If you don't see any signs of interest in a specific topic, you can try interesting your child in something by doing one of the following:

- ❏ Read a book
- ❏ Watch a video
- ❏ Show him concrete objects
- ❏ Talk about a topic
- ❏ Vist a place where you can observe or see objects or things
- ❏ Share your own interest in a topic

Be sure to choose a topic that your child wants to know about! Without your child's interest, it will not become a project. Be sure to take time to find something that your child wants to know about.

Parent Journal: *What is my child interested in? What does he want to know about?*

HOW TO DECIDE IF AN INTEREST IS A GOOD PROJECT TOPIC

1. *A good project topic includes real objects.* Children enjoy touching, moving, and using real objects in their play. Children learn by touching, moving, carrying, modeling, hearing, tasting, and looking closely. Choose a project topic that has many real things that are safe to handle, not just ideas. For example, fire trucks is a better project than fire fighting; mirrors is a better topic than reflections.

2. *A good project topic is connected to something your child knows about.* Children like to learn about things they already know something about. It is hard for young children to think about topics for which they have little experience or words. Boats might be a good topic if your child has been in a real boat but not so good if he has never seen a boat. Think about your child's daily life. What does he see? Where does she go? What is around your neighborhood? For example, the ocean is not a good topic if you live in the middle of the United States.

3. *A good project topic can be investigated at a place you can visit,* preferably again and again. Children, especially young children, benefit from seeing real places. If a child can only learn about something from books or photos he can develop unrealistic ideas. For example, studying the ocean without ever visiting it might result in a number of misunderstandings. Think broadly about places to visit. A field-site visit might be a short walk to your garage or to the shop at the end of your street. Your child will also benefit by going to places again and again. When you first take your child to the zoo, he may have difficulty focusing on just the monkeys, but after a visit or two the rest of the zoo won't be so distracting. When you choose a topic for project work, think about where you might visit. Learning how your lawnmower works might be a better topic than studying airplanes, which requires a trip to the airport, because you can easily go to see a real lawnmower and you can do it over and over again.

4. *A good project topic can be researched by your child.* Research for young children consists of observing, manipulating, experimenting, asking questions, trying out ideas, and visiting places. Young children are less interested when they have to listen or learn only through books, videos, encyclopedias, or what an adult tells them. Your child will learn more when she can "study" a topic herself (touch, poke, turn, etc.). It works best if you can be a resource and help your child rather than be a lecturer on the topic.

5. *A good project topic enables your child to use skills and methods appropriate for his age.* Children like to share what they know through drawings, paintings, sculptures, or playing. Young children especially like to make play places, such as a McDonald's restaurant, where they can pretend. Is there something that your child could draw, paint, make a model of, or use for pretend play?

6. *A good project topic is worth studying.* Projects take time and effort; so, what children study should be worth learning about. For example, learning the characters in a favorite video may be interesting, but it won't help develop school skills or interest in school subjects. It would be better to learn how a car works or what happens in a grocery store than to do a project on a movie character. This is especially true if interest in school is an issue with your child.

7. *A good project topic is related to your child's world.* Projects should help children learn about their daily world and their family and community. The world of young children is very small—family, neighborhood, and school or care center. Projects that are based on family interests are especially meaningful. If there is a family tradition of fishing, and many adults in your family fish, this could be a great project.

Parent Journal: *Mess around with the topic. What happened? Is my child still interested?*

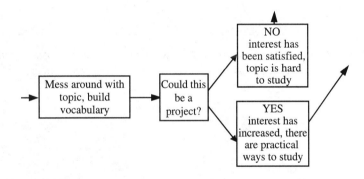

Parent Journal: *Is this a good topic for us to consider as a project? Why or why not?*

FIND OUT WHAT YOUR CHILD
UNDERSTANDS ABOUT THE TOPIC

The more you talk about the topic with your child, the more you will know what your child might have questions about. This will give you ideas of whom to talk to and where you might like to visit.

What does my child know about this topic?

You can keep a record of what he knows and what he learns by
• Making a web
• Making a list of questions
• Saving drawings
• Photographing things he builds
• Writing down what he says

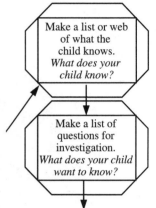

Parent Journal: *Record what your child knows about this topic. What words, ideas, and understandings does my child have?*

FORM QUESTIONS FOR INVESTIGATING

It is important for your child to find answers to her own questions. Your child may surprise you with what she wants to know. For example, she may want to know where the fire-fighter eats his dinner or what the fisherman does with his fish. Because you want your child to **think,** it is important that she research what **she** wants to find out. This is how you can support the development of your child's curiosity and intellectual dispositions.

You can help your child learn to form a question by doing the following:

Looking at a book on the topic, you could say (fill in the blanks appropriately for your topic):

What things in that picture do you want to know about? What is _____?

Where do you think _____? Would you like to know that?

Who do you think that is? Would you like to know who does _____?

When do you think the _____ does _____?

Why do they _____? Why does he _____?

You can also model questions.
I would like to know what that is. I would like to know what that is used for.
I wonder how the mechanic gets rusted bolts off of the car.

Parent Journal: *What questions does my child have about this topic?*

SETTING THE STAGE

As you prepare for the investigation phase, you will have a number of considerations about the work environment, materials, and time. Each of these issues can be addressed with thoughtful planning and organization.

1. How can I provide an environment for meaningful learning?
   - ❑ Where is there enough space for my child and me to work together?
   - ❑ Where will I be comfortable working alongside my child?
   - ❑ Where will my child have a surface to write, draw, paint, and use materials like clay?

2. As you prepare to gather materials you will need for project work, the following questions will help you collect basic supplies and tools you will need.
   - ❑ What will we write and draw with?(ex. markers, chalk, crayons, pens, pencils)
   - ❑ What will we write and draw on? (ex. paper, chalkboard, old envelopes, note cards)
   - ❑ What will we paint with? (ex. sponges, brushes)
   - ❑ What will we use to hold things together? (ex. glue, tape, tacky glue, staples, brads)
   - ❑ What will we cut with? (ex. child scissors, adult scissors)
   - ❑ What will we use to sculpt? (ex. clay, wire, play dough)
   - ❑ What will use to clean up our mess? (ex. paper towels, sponges, baby wipes)

3. How can I store materials for projects and other forms of meaningful learning?
   - ❑ Where will we keep paper, clay, and books about project topics?
   - ❑ Where can ongoing work be stored so that it is safe from siblings, vacuum cleaners, or the dog?
   - ❑ Where can materials be stored neatly and safely but so that they are still accessible to my child?

4. How will I prepare a literacy-rich environment for project work?
   - ❑ Where is a flat surface for writing and drawing with enough room to lay out reference books?
   - ❑ Do I have writing tools like pens, pencils, fine-line markers, and colored pencils readily available to encourage writing?
   - ❑ Do I have different kinds and sizes of writing paper for writing, making signs, and labeling readily available to encourage writing?
   - ❑ Do I have a picture dictionary?
   - ❑ Do I have a tub, basket, or shelf that can be used just for books on project topics?
   - ❑ Where can I go to get reference books? Do I know where my library is located, and do I have a card?
   - ❑ Where can I get on the Internet to get information for my child?

5. How can I provide the time for projects and other forms of meaningful learning?
   - ❑ When can we reserve time so we can really concentrate on our project work?
   - ❑ Are there short blocks of time when we could fit in project work, such as a stop at the library or a drawing session?

6. How will I document my child's learning?
   - ❑ Do I have a camera or video camera to record field sites and my child's work?
   - ❑ Do I have a place to display my child's work?
   - ❑ How will I keep a history of the project?

Teaching Your Child to Love Learnng, Copyright © 2004 by Teachers College, Columbia University

MATERIALS AND SUPPLIES

As you begin your collection of materials, check out the following list to see what you might currently have at home and what items you might want to purchase or borrow. Keep in mind that you will never need all of these items for every project. Different projects will lend themselves to the use of different materials.

Aluminum foil	Fabric	Q-tips
Art smock	Feathers	Ribbon
Balloons	Felt	Rubber bands
Balls	Film canisters	Ruler
Beads	Foam	Scissors
Beans	Glitter	Sponges
Bottle caps	Glue	Stapler
Boxes	Hole punch	Stencils
Brads	Lace	String
Buttons	Lids	Tape—clear, packing
Cardboard	Masking tape	Thread
Ceramic tiles	Nails	Tissue paper
Chalk	Newspaper	Toothpicks
Clay	Noodles, dry	Wallpaper scraps
Clothespins	Markers—thin, fat	Wrapping paper
Coffee filters	Modeling clay (e.g., Sculpey)	Yarn
Construction paper	Paint—tempera, watercolors	
Cotton balls	Pencils	Additional ideas:
Crepe paper	Pipe cleaners	
Egg cartons	Popsicle sticks	

As you explore your topic, children will often need a medium to sculpt or mold. While many commercial materials such as Model Magic by Crayola or Sculpey modeling compound can be purchased, you may want to consider using the simple, homemade play dough recipe below.

Homemade Play Dough Recipe*

2 cups of flour
1 cup of salt
A few drops of food coloring

2 tablespoons of alum (do not substitute)
2 cups of boiling water

1. Mix the dry ingredients in a mixing bowl. Put water on to boil and add the food coloring to the water.
2. Add the boiling water to the dry ingredients. Allow the water to soak in for a couple of minutes while it cools.
3. After a few minutes, begin to knead the mixture. The more you knead the dough, the smoother the consistency will be. Store in an airtight container.

*Be very exact in the measurements

Phase Two

INVESTIGATING YOUR TOPIC

WHAT DO YOU HOPE YOUR CHILD WILL LEARN?

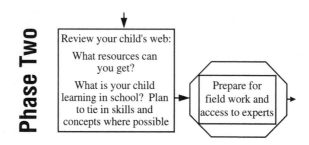

There is one last thing for you to do before you begin the most exciting phase of the project work, investigation. Take some time to think about what you want your child to learn from this experience.

Parent Journal: *What do I hope my child will learn from these investigations?*

PREPARE FOR FIELD WORK

Now is the time to think about places that you can visit with your child to investigate this topic. Where could you go to learn?

How will I help my child focus his investigation?
- ❏ Discussion ❏ List of questions ❏ List of tasks to do

This is when you will help your child learn new information about the topic and get her questions answered. You may visit a place; have conversations with someone who has expertise; and collect real objects, books, or photographs. A field-site visit provides a shared event. You can coach your child in using the skills of observing, talking, drawing, painting, and sketching. Encourage your child to ask the questions the two of you prepared.

You may want to think how you can prepare your child for this experience:
- ❏ Discuss it with her in advance
- ❏ Practice skills such as drawing or photographing
- ❏ Remind your child about the purpose of the visit and about the questions
- ❏ Rehearse asking questions

Parent Journal: *What specific experiences do I want my child to have on a field-site visit? What specific discoveries do I want to occur?*

IDENTIFYING AND FINDING EXPERTS

In good project work, children interact with adults (or even older children) to find answers to their questions and to learn from them. An "expert" in project work refers to anyone who has more knowledge about the topic than the child. It is more important to find experts who can talk to the child on her level than to find experts with "recognized expertise." For example, Uncle Harry, who has a new pick up truck and is interested in talking about trucks with your child, would be a better expert than a community college automotive instructor.

What expertise do we need for this project? What does someone need to know about this topic to be an expert for my child?
- ❏ What skills will the expert be able to share?
- ❏ Does he have real objects that he could lend to my child for investigation?
- ❏ Does she have time to spend with my family?
- ❏ Is he up to the activity level involved? (For example, Grandpa may be able to give great advice regarding fishing lures but not be able to hike along a trout stream.)
- ❏ Is this person someone I want my child to spend time with? (Experts are often seen as role models. It is wise to think about this when establishing contact.)

Parent Journal: *What kind of "expert" do we need? Where might I find one?*

TAKING YOUR CHILD ON A FIELD EXPERIENCE

Do I need to arrange for transportation to a site? Do I need to let the appropriate person at the site know we are coming? How can I let him know what my child is studying and what we want to know?

1 to 2 weeks before the visit:
Do I need to
      ❏ Phone the site   or   ❏ Scout it out
      ❏ Prepare a sibling to go along   or   ❏ Arrange for care of siblings

Think about discussing with your field-site expert
_____ Safety issues involved in this site visit or expert visit
_____ Importance of your child investigating and being able to ask questions
_____ Overview of what your child currently knows and understands and what she is interested in learning
_____ Importance of concrete real objects, especially those that your child can interact with
_____ How your child will be recording what she learns—
      Tape recording? Video? Clipboards? Writing? Photographing?
_____ Items or scenes that your child may want to spend some time sketching, recording, etc. (Be sure to allow enough time in your visit for sketching, manipulating real objects, etc. Plan the visit so your child does not feel hurried.)
_____ Any tools, equipment, products, etc. that can be borrowed for further investigation

Notes:

On the day of the visit:
Materials and supplies needed:
_____ Clipboards
_____ Recording equipment: ❏ camera   ❏ video   ❏ tape recorder
_____ Paper, pencils, art materials
_____ Bags, boxes, or other containers for materials collected
_____ Other

As your child investigates and visits field sites, she may develop new questions. You may need to provide additional resources to meet this need.

Parent Journal: *What additional questions does my child have?*

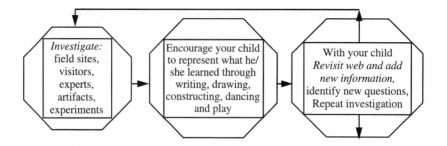

HELPING YOUR CHILD REPRESENT WHAT HE IS LEARNING

How will my child review his experiences and field work?

❏ Discuss sketches　　❏ Time 1/Time 2 drawings　　❏ Review photos　　❏ Dictate experience

❏ Revise webs　　❏ List answers to questions　　❏ Scrapbook　　❏ Display

How will I focus my child on other resources?

❏ Introduce new books　　❏ Add more concrete things related to the topic　　❏ Encourage play

How can my child represent what he has learned about the topic?

❏ Drawings/ sketches　　❏ Paintings　　❏ Constructions　　❏ Play　　❏ Language products

What do I need to do to encourage representation?

How can I foster the following experiences through this project?

❏ Problem Solving: What can my child figure out on his own?

❏ Development of construction skills such as taping, gluing, and organizing materials?

Parent Journal: If your child is school age, what school skills might be used in this project?

Reading:

Writing and spelling:

Math:

Science or social studies:

What additional resources can you bring into your home so that your child can find more information and learn at a deeper level of study?
❏ Books
❏ Construction Materials
❏ Adults to interview
❏ Objects to play with and take apart

Is there one aspect or part of the topic that your child seems especially interested in, such as a part of a car or the checkout scanner? Can you study this aspect or object in more depth?

Phase Three

CELEBRATING THE LEARNING

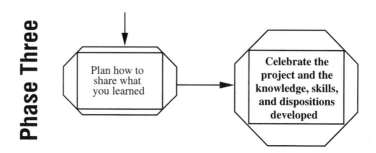

Phase Three

Plan how to share what you learned → Celebrate the project and the knowledge, skills, and dispositions developed

All projects come to an end. This is a natural process. Some projects will be short, while other projects may extend for months. It is time to end a project when you can answer "yes" to any of these questions:

_____ Is my child satisfied with what she has learned about the topic?

_____ Would further investigation require more skills than my child can learn at this age—such as car repair or driving

_____ Has my child lost interest in the topic?

WHY WE CULMINATE AND CELEBRATE

Although all projects eventually end, they should be celebrated in some way. Looking back at what has been learned and accomplished in a project builds your child's self-confidence. It helps your child identify what it means to learn and the feelings of satisfaction that come from learning. Celebrating provides a sense of closure. The process of celebrating can create memories that will be treasured for years to come.

Don't be surprised if your child's interest wanes and she doesn't finish a project. Remember the important thing is that the child **thinks, investigates, and sees herself as a learner.** It is not necessary for children to finish every project. Young children will explore lots of interests before they find what they especially like. When they do a project, interest in the topic can last for years and even become a vocation.

EVIDENCE OF LEARNING

It is helpful to take time to make a collection of what your child has learned and what skills she has developed. This can be documented by

❏ Drawings/sketches ❏ Webs ❏ Paintings
❏ Lists ❏ Constructions ❏ Murals
❏ Play ❏ Photographs ❏ Making a collection
❏ Language products (such as writing diagrams, charts, posters)

CELEBRATE THE PROJECT

Projects usually end with some way to capture and remember the experience. Your child may

- Make models
- Start a scrapbook
- Play out the experience (while you take photos)
- Start a collection
- Paint pictures
- Take photos
- Draw pictures
- Make a video
- Share what he has learned with neighbors and friends
- Present what he has learned to his class at school

Young children won't know how to do these things the first time, and you will have to help your child make a scrapbook or show him how he can collect items. Remember, however, to let your child take the lead. The scrapbook may not be neat or the model may not look much like the real thing. It is important, however, that your child do the work and feel good about the experience.

Parent Journal: Culminating the project. What ways might I help my child culminate this project so that we all have a sense of accomplishment?

THE NEXT PROJECT

Parent Journal: Is there another topic that has emerged for further investigation? Could we investigate this topic now or at a later time?

LAST THOUGHT FOR PARENTS

Parent Journal: What did I learn from sharing this experience with my child? What did I learn about my child's strengths and interests? How might I support my child's meaningful learning in the future?

Teaching Your Child to Love Learnng, Copyright © 2004 by Teachers College, Columbia University